THE SHORTEST HISTORY OF MUSIC

Other Titles in the Shortest History Series

The Shortest History of China by Linda Jaivin
The Shortest History of the Crown by Stephen Bates
The Shortest History of Democracy by John Keane
The Shortest History of Economics by Andrew Leigh
The Shortest History of India by John Zubrzycki
The Shortest History of Israel and Palestine by Michael Scott-Baumann
The Shortest History of Sex by David Baker
The Shortest History of the Soviet Union by Sheila Fitzpatrick
The Shortest History of the Universe by David Baker
The Shortest History of War by Gwynne Dyer

Also by Andrew Ford

The Song Remains the Same: 800 Years of Love Songs, Laments and Lullabies (with Anni Heino) (2019)
The Memory of Music (2017)
Earth Dances: Music in Search of the Primitive (2015)
Try Whistling This: Writings About Music (2012)
The Sound of Pictures: Listening to the Movies, from Hitchcock to High Fidelity (2010)
Talking to Kinky and Karlheinz: 170 Musicians Get Vocal on The Music Show (ed. Anni Heino) (2008)
In Defence of Classical Music (2005)
Speaking in Tongues: The Songs of Van Morrison (with Martin Buzacott) (2005)
Undue Noise: Words About Music (2002)
Illegal Harmonies: Music in the Modern Age (1997, 2011)
Composer to Composer: Conversations about Contemporary Music (1993)

PRAISE FOR *THE SHORTEST HISTORY OF MUSIC*

'An absolute belter … this is just a marvellous book.'
—ABC Radio Illawarra

'Andrew Ford is a brilliant guide to the inner sanctums of composition and the outer reaches of what we can even call music … *The Shortest History of Music* is for every music lover.' —*Tasmanian Times*

'It may be a miniature, but this story of music strikes the right note … The book's chief delight is its constant asides, tangents and anecdotes, which appear on almost every page.' —*The Age*

'*The Shortest History of Music* is an achievement in brevity and balance – the well-themed structure providing steady tack through the surging and sometimes rough seas of musical history … Note to prospective readers: stop and listen to any piece that is mentioned more than once. It will deepen the experience profoundly.'
—*The Saturday Paper*

'Like an experienced jazz player, [Ford] knows how to swing his narrative, with delightful off-road lurches into unexpected or cheeky byways.'
—*Australian Book Review*

'In the latest in the admirable Shortest History series, [Andrew Ford] considers the impulse to make music, notated music, music as a commodity, modernism and music, and the consequences of recording. All that in about 250 pages.' —*The Sydney Morning Herald*

'It is impossible to convey enough of the substance and value of this small treasure.'
—Queensland Reviewers Collective

'*The Shortest History of Music* by Andrew Ford demonstrates why music is so critical to understanding the human condition.' —*The Weekend Australian*

THE SHORTEST HISTORY OF MUSIC

ANDREW FORD

PICADOR INDIA

First published in Australia in 2024 by Black Inc.
First published in India 2025 by Picador India
an imprint of Pan Macmillan Publishing India Private Limited
707 Kailash Building
26 K. G. Marg, New Delhi 110001
www.panmacmillan.co.in

Pan Macmillan, The Smithson, 6 Briset Street, Farringdon, London EC1M 5NR
Associated companies throughout the world
www.panmacmillan.com

ISBN 978-93-6113-316-9

1 3 5 7 9 8 6 4 2

Printed and bound in India by Thomson Press India Ltd.

FSC www.fsc.org
MIX
Paper | Supporting responsible forestry
FSC® C010615

For Anni and Elsie with love

Contents

Introduction 1

1. The Tradition of Music: from Prehistory to the Present 7
2. Music and Notation: Blueprints for Building in Sound from 1400 BCE to the Present 47
3. Music for Sale: Paying the Piper from 1000 BCE to the Present 89
4. Music and Modernism: Reinventing the Art from 1150 to the Present 137
5. Recording Music: from 1900 to the Present 187

Epilogue: What Is Music? 205

Further Reading 211
Acknowledgements 219
Image Credits 221
Index 223

Introduction

IN 1987 OR THEREABOUTS, William Barton, a Kalkadunga boy in the Gulf country of Northwest Queensland, went with his father in search of a tree that might make a didgeridoo.

'You know what trees to look for,' the adult Barton remembered. 'There's coolibah trees, there's snappy gum, there's bloodwood, and also there's gidgee, which is a really hard wood around the Mount Isa area. I just went walkabout. I was looking for a nice deep didgeridoo, a long one with a big diameter that would give a deep tone when you played it. You can usually tell just from looking at the tree what key the didgeridoo is going to be in.'

The word 'didgeridoo' (sometimes spelt 'didjeridu') has a disputed origin that, whatever else it may be, is not Aboriginal. There are at least fifty words for the instrument in the Indigenous languages of northern Australia, including 'ilpirra' in the Arrernte language, 'yidaki' in Yolŋu and 'garbak' in Gagadju.

Although the first peoples of Australia have been on the island continent for around 70,000 years, archaeological evidence can only date the instrument to a thousand years ago. After all, wood rots. But even if it were only one millennium old, we may speculate that as enslaved Cham women sang and danced for the Vietnamese emperor Lý Thái Tông at his court in the middle of the eleventh century; as the Abbess Hildegard led a choir of Benedictine nuns through one of her newly composed sequences at the Abbey of Eibingen on the Rhine in the late twelfth century; as Amīr Khusrau developed the Sufi devotional style of singing known as qawwali in the Delhi Sultanate at the end of the thirteenth century; as Thomas Tallis composed a grand forty-part motet in London sometime before 1570; as Joseph Haydn donned his servant's uniform at Esterháza in the late 1700s; as Clara Schumann invented the piano recital and with it helped cement the notion of Western classical music nearly a century later; as, fifty years on, recently emancipated African Americans picked up the discarded instruments of Civil War marching bands and began to play jazz, somewhere in northern Australia, a young boy and his father would have been out looking for a likely tree.

Alongside any history of change there will always be continuity.

On the face of it, a history of music is an obvious subject for a book. For much of the twentieth century, Western schools and universities taught music – which is to say Western art music – as though it *was* history. Bach and Handel led to Haydn, Mozart and Beethoven, who led to Schubert, Robert Schumann and Mendelssohn, who led to Wagner and Brahms. It is significant that these composers were Germans or Austrians to a man (and that's significant, too). Of course there were non-Germanic composers – Berlioz, Chopin and Liszt; Tchaikovsky, Dvořák, Elgar and Sibelius; Verdi in the opera house – but they weren't quite the main game. The standard view was that 'classical music' was a German thing and that it had gone on for about two hundred years. Everything before Bach and Handel was 'early music'; everything after Brahms was 'modern'. Among the modern composers were such thorny propositions as Schoenberg, Bartók and Stravinsky, but also Debussy and Ravel, whose music was less prickly and possibly less substantial, the term 'impressionist' that was unthinkingly applied to the French composers always seeming a little dismissive.

That all these European composers were men was seldom remarked upon and, in the eighteenth and nineteenth centuries, perhaps not so noteworthy. After all, the proportion of women to men in the composition profession – and it *was* a profession – was much the same as in law, medicine, commerce and politics. Dismantling the patriarchy still has some way to go.

The notion of classical music as history – where one thing leads to another, where there's evolution and occasionally revolution, where there's progress – remains seductive, and one can see how it came about. All music is a form of knowledge, but Western art music actually *looks* like knowledge because it comes in books. Since this music is notated, it is easy to pick up a chorale by J.S. Bach, study it and sing it; and for a later composer to write music that draws on Bach's example or does something completely different. As a way of understanding this music, the historicist's approach is not entirely unhelpful, and it would be a mistake to write it off. But it offers a limited and partial view of just some of the world's music. For other sorts of music, it hardly holds at all.

Even written-down music is hard to put into words. Music that is not written down but either part of an oral tradition or spontaneously improvised is harder still. Unless it is recorded, it disappears in an instant. The most you can hope for is that it 'vibrates in the memory', as the poet Shelley put it. When it comes to writing its history, then, we continually run up against this problem: about Western art music we know a lot, and we have ready access to a vast amount of the music itself; with nearly all the other music in the world (prior to the advent of recording), we know a lot less, and have access to virtually none of it. We may see the art and architecture of ancient civilisations and we may attempt to decipher their writings; we may not hear their music.

And there is another problem to do with the notion of history in relation to music. The jazz trumpeter and composer Wynton Marsalis once insisted that all jazz is modern because it is continually being made, existing in an endless present tense. This might be said of music in general, and (as the philosopher Benedetto Croce suggested) history in general. The young William Barton's search for the right tree was symbolic of this, and so is our singing of a Bach chorale, our twenty-first-century voices breathing new life into music imagined and composed some three hundred years earlier, the music reborn in each fresh performance.

With music, we are always going back to the start, the plainest evidence of which is the pre-verbal squeals and gurgles of a baby, sometimes playful, sometimes urgently communicative, often both. It's proto-music, and that's where this history must begin. How it should continue is a trickier matter.

In some form, music is happening all around us all the time, its ubiquity throughout human existence making it impossible to track in any linear sense. Accordingly, this book considers its subject thematically in five main chapters.

The impulse to make music, whether to celebrate some great occasion or to soothe a child to sleep, is basic to us, and the first chapter looks at examples of this impulse from prehistory to the present in numerous different cultures. In particular, it examines the ways in which musical types and styles and musical instruments have travelled between cultures. Traditional music depends on memory, but notated music, which is the subject of Chapter Two, allows complex music to be repeated and, significantly, to be planned by composers in order to produce musical works of a grand scale. Chapter Three examines how, since David composed his psalms in the temple (and probably before), musicians have plied their trades and how music itself has been bought and sold as a commodity. In Chapter Four, the twentieth-century concept of 'modernism' is traced back to medieval Europe, the desire to be modern a form of tradition in notated and, more recently, recorded music. Recording itself is considered in the final chapter, its effect, in little more than a century, to have expanded the availability of music on a previously unimaginable scale, but also to change the way music is made.

Because no history of music – let alone the shortest – can hope to be comprehensive, I have chosen my examples for the general story they tell, and brought back certain figures and pieces of music not because this composer or that piece is the greatest of their time and place, but because they explain the uses of music and ways in which it has changed. Above all, I have been at pains to address music on the smallest scale as well as the largest, considering not only famous names and famous works, but also domestic music. That is, after all, how music started and how it will start again tomorrow.

1

THE TRADITION OF MUSIC: FROM PREHISTORY TO THE PRESENT

ALTHOUGH MUSIC IS AS INTRINSIC to human life as the air we breathe, we must never fall for the line that it is a universal language. Music is neither universal, nor a language.

The use of the word 'universal' suggests that all music speaks equally to all people. Clearly, it does not. While music might be everywhere, no one appreciates all of it and often enough the barrier to appreciation is cultural. American country music, Italian baroque arias, Indian ragas, hip hop, twelve-tone string quartets: everyone can name a form of music that leaves them unmoved and possibly drives them mad – assuming, that is, they can agree on what constitutes music in the first place. In most of the indigenous languages of Africa, although there are words for performing, for singing and dancing, for drumming and playing other instruments, there is no equivalent word for music.

Were music a language, it could be translated into other

languages. But that is not how music works. Music might be good at generating emotion, but it can tell you nothing precise: a shopping list, a set of directions, a love letter are all beyond it. Music communicates nothing; it *is* something.

* * *

> I think music is the art of agony. Music is, after all, derived from screaming; it is not derived from laughing.
>
> —Percy Grainger (1882–1961),
> Australian composer

Music is a precursor to language. It is not that it predates language in the historical sense (though it probably does), but that a version of music comes out of the mouths of babes and sucklings before they are able to form words. Some of a baby's cries will have to do with hunger or the desire for company, but there are also moments when the infant lies there experimenting with sound for its own sake, and that is music. Why do babies do this? We know that children learn through imitation and that this begins at about six months. They respond to the sounds around them, including birds and animals; they imitate the voices of their parents and siblings; and they form a particularly strong bond – a musical bond – with the parent who sings. Originally, perhaps, this 'singing' consisted of cooing reassuring tones, and it can still be that. Archaeological evidence suggests that *Homo erectus* – the ancestor of both human beings and Neanderthals – had the facial bone structure to make different pitches.

A rudimentary form of music having come first in a child's development, the words that follow gain meaning from pitch, rhythm, tempo, timbre and emphasis – the component parts of music. With tonal languages, such as Vietnamese, Cherokee and Yoruba (spoken in much of Nigeria and Benin), infants learn relative pitches or pitch shapes as part of pronunciation. Chinese children learning Mandarin must differentiate between four tonal shapes, a single syllable having completely unrelated meanings depending upon whether the pitch is high and straight, rising, falling then rising, or abruptly falling. So *mā* means mother, *má* means cannabis, *mǎ* is a horse and *mà* is the verb to scold or curse (and, what's more, context is important, because *má* also means leprosy, while *mǎ* can mean agate). Even in non-tonal languages, such as English, pitch remains important as speaking voices rise and fall to indicate sense. Our speech slows down and speeds up; it grows louder or quieter, softer or gruffer; we stress certain words and not others, creating free-flowing rhythmic patterns. We do all this at the service of the words we utter, the *music* of our voices allowing those we are talking to to understand the nuances of meaning and gauge veracity. If you want to know whether your new hairdo looks good, you will have to listen to the *way* your interlocutor says, 'Oh, it really suits you.'

So, music is both more primitive than speech and a part of speech. Crucially, music can also be a step up from speech when the rhythms and pitches of vocal communication are exaggerated into song. Vowels are extended and perhaps decorated with more than one note; important syllables are placed on strong beats and high notes. Song is stylised speaking, although precise distinctions will vary from culture to culture.

Is this, then, how music began? With singing? It's tempting to believe so. But perhaps even before people sang, they made rhythms. Consciously or not, we do this all the time: we do it when we walk; even asleep, our breathing and heartbeat create patterns in sound. Early hominins must have noticed this. Stone tools date back more than two million years, and their use would have generated rhythm. Working together, our ancestors created spontaneous polyphony, or perhaps, listening to each other, their hammering fell pleasingly into step. The patterns might have been basic and almost unconscious, but as soon as people pay attention to one another's rhythms and interact with them, they are making music.

* * *

> The way music passes, emblematic
> Of life and how you cannot isolate a note of it
> And say it is good or bad. You must
> Wait till it's over.
>
> —from 'Syringa' by
> John Ashbery (1927–2017), American poet

The cognitive psychologist Steven Pinker, who has written on rationality and humankind's instinct for language, has tended to pooh-pooh music. Because music isn't a language, and since it is hard to say in what sense it might be entirely rational, Pinker regards it as something of an outlier, 'an exquisite confection crafted to tickle the sensitive spots of at least six of our mental faculties' but conferring 'no survival advantage'. Music is all very nice, but it doesn't matter; it is, in Pinker's view, the auditory equivalent of 'cheesecake'.

Now, just because something can't be explained in words does not make it unimportant. On the contrary, it may be *because* music is so hard to pin down that it has been valued throughout history. The sites of archaeological finds place musical instruments in temples, royal tombs and inner sanctums at the heart of cave systems; early visual depictions of music-making show people playing instruments for kings and queens and gods. But alongside what we might think of as these high-end uses of music, there must always have been the crooning parent. From ancient times, music was part of life at every level.

It was the ancient Greeks who invented cheesecake, so it is conceivable that Pythagoras, Socrates, Plato and Aristotle were all partial to it. In any case, these philosophers would have made short shrift of Steven Pinker and his theory. Music had a vital importance not only in the Greeks' individual lives, but also at the level of government, and it involved choral singing and dance as well as lyric poems, sung or chanted to the accompaniment of a lyre. What are now generally considered separate disciplines – music, dance and poetry – to the Greeks were one thing (they still are for many First Nations peoples). Even so, Pythagoras found a certain purity in musical sounds born of the mathematical proportions of the harmonic series – the way, for example, a vibrating string half the length of another vibrating string will produce a tone one octave higher. Music, Pythagoras believed, was a key to the cosmos and vice versa.

For Socrates, far from being Pinker's 'exquisite confection', music wasn't even about enjoyment but the bestowing of order – although, recognising music's power to beguile and make the listener lazy, he recommended its teaching alongside gymnastics. Plato, in his *Laws*, suggested that music – in particular choric music (dancing as well as singing) – might be employed to calm youthful hotheads and bring discipline to their minds; and he goes further, for in *The Republic* he asserts that the power of music is that it bypasses reason, going straight to the soul or self. Both Plato and Aristotle were somewhat disapproving of purely instrumental music, as many societies have been, especially religious societies. But singing for Plato was such a serious matter that he proposed putting the laws of the state to music.

* * *

> We see how the songspirals can be destroyed. If
> Yolŋu all die, then the land dies with us.
>
> —from *Songspirals* by the Gay'wu Group of Women

For the Yolŋu people of northeast Arnhem Land, songs embody law and lore. The Gay'wu Group of Women, who write so vividly about this, prefer the term 'songspirals' to the more common expression 'songlines' because their 'songs are not a straight line . . . [moving] in one direction through time and space'. For Yolŋu people, these songspirals not only come from the land; they are continually forming it.

Yolŋu women have responsibility for milkarri, which 'is an ancient song, an ancient poem, a map, a ceremony and a guide, but it is more than all this too'. When they sing – or cry, or keen – milkarri, they are forming a connection to clan, to family and to homeland, 'to the waters and rocks and winds and animals, to everything'.

'When we do milkarri,' the Gay'wu Group of Women say, 'as soon as we hear it, the tears just come, because the words and the meanings are so deep that the land is talking. It is our cry for her people and the people are crying for the land. Country cries too. It has its milkarri. We keen milkarri for Country and Country keens its milkarri with us.'

What the Gay'wu women describe here could hardly be further from Pinker's cheesecake theory. The women's singing is vital and important; it grounds them in time and place. The music embodies meaning, not only because the melodic lines carry words, but also because the two are fused, the music coming to stand for those words.

The putting of music to words – and words to music – is, we may presume, as old as language itself, and enables music to form a clear connection to the extra-musical world, telling a story, giving praise, sharing grief or joy. In cultures that don't use written language, it becomes a repository of lore and a form of mass media. Without words, music is harder to pin down, but it can still gain non-musical meaning and social significance by dint of prior agreement. An example of this might be the blowing of the shofar (ram's horn) in Jewish tradition, and here one can hardly speak of music per se. It is the sound of the shofar that is significant, coupled with the signals it plays: a long note (tekiah), three continuous long notes (shevarim) and ten or more short notes (teruah), heard in various combinations. The shofar is blown after morning services (except on the Sabbath) during the month of Elul leading up to Rosh Hashanah (New Year), when it is sounded 100 or 101 times; it is also heard at the end of Yom Kippur (the Day of Atonement). It has a political function, too, being blown following the swearing in of an Israeli president, a tradition dating back to biblical times, when the shofar announced that a king had been anointed.

In the Book of Exodus, the blasts from a shofar emanating 'exceeding loud' from the clouds on Mount Sinai made the Israelites tremble in the camp below, and that ability to send signals with clarity and high volume over a distance was surely among the earliest uses of musical instruments, calling people together, alerting them to danger, giving directions in hunting or in battle.

These examples of the power of pitch and timbre and rhythm are specific and cultural. They help to define, reinforce and bind together those who produce the musical sounds and those who hear them. At some level this is what all music does, whether ancient or modern, traditional or innovative, sacred or secular. Even commercial pop music can take on this function, a playlist forming a kind of musical representation of the listener's identity.

Music's ubiquity is a sign of its enduring importance; from the earliest times music was passed from one generation to another and also between states and cultures, shared by traders and diplomats, imposed by invaders or preserved in the memories of enslaved people as a cultural remnant. Instruments and instrumental designs, likewise, crossed oceans. Most of the world's peoples have drums and other percussion, most have stringed instruments for plucking or bowing or both, and nearly all have flutes and other wind instruments.

* * *

> There is no reason why high-born flute players should receive the best instruments, for they will not play any better. The superior instrument should be reserved for the superior player.
>
> —from *Politics* by Aristotle (384–322 BCE)

We don't know how well they were played or by whom, but flutes provide the earliest archaeological evidence of music on our planet. The instruments are made of bone and some of them are more than 40,000 years old. A particularly delicate example, made from a vulture's bone, was unearthed in a cave in the Swabian Jura of southern Germany in 2008. Beside it were fragments of larger flutes made of mammoth tusk.

While we can only imagine the sounds of the flutes and the nature of the music they played, the location of the site seems significant, for the instruments were found in a cave that had an especially advantageous acoustic, a reverberant space that might have amplified the sounds throughout the cave system or even formed a small 'concert hall'. As with so much in archaeology, we are dealing in speculation.

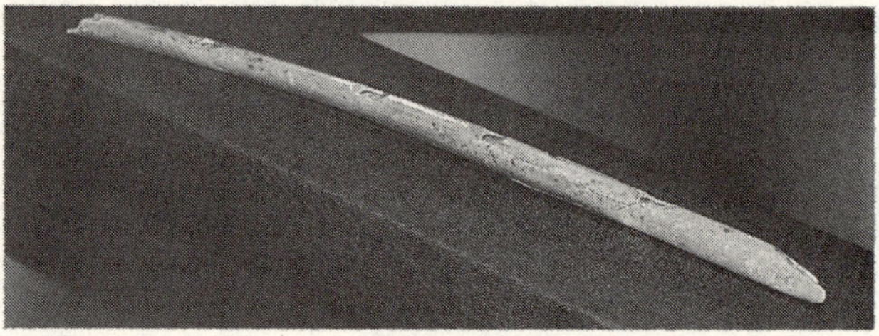

Bone flute made from a vulture's wing

Bone flutes of this sort – tubes with holes, end-blown like a penny whistle – are relatively simple instruments, though their manufacture, by early human-Neanderthal hybrids using stone implements, remains a marvel. Sometimes, however, it is hard to say how the holes were made. A short length of bear femur found in northwestern Slovenia in 1995 is approximately 20,000 years older than the German instruments. It features what appear to be two finger holes, and the fragment, when reconstructed, has been held by some to be part of a flute capable of playing a diatonic scale. Plenty of experts have insisted that the holes were made by an animal, but, if it really were a flute, the instrument would have been made around

60,000 BCE, the Middle Palaeolithic period, and it would be the work of Neanderthals.

Bianzhong from the tomb of Marquis Yi of Zeng

Flute-making is a relatively sophisticated art compared to the construction of a simple drum, so it's hard to believe drums didn't exist first. The fact that we have no drum anything as old as the bone flutes is down to the relative biodegradability of the materials involved – bone lasts longer than skin and wood. The earliest surviving drums had bodies made of clay and heads of alligator skin. They have been discovered at Neolithic sites across China and date from roughly 5500 to 3000 BCE. Later drums have been found with wooden frames. The Bronze Age brought bronze drums and gongs in southern China and Southeast Asia, perhaps most famously the Vietnamese đông sơn drums, prized as artefacts as much as musical instruments, and the Chinese bianzhong, a rack of tuned bronze bells. A set of sixty-four was found at Hubei in the tomb of Marquis Yi of Zeng (the marquis died in 433 BCE). Metal casting also allowed the manufacture of horns, originally, as the word suggests, made from animal horns. Tutankhamun's tomb (1323 BCE) in Egypt contained trumpets in bronze and silver.

The earliest existing harps and lyres, dating from around 2500 BCE, were unearthed at Sumer in ancient Mesopotamia (today, south-central Iraq) and further south at royal burial chambers in Ur (Tell el-Muqayyar). The earliest surviving zither is a Chinese qin – or guqin, to give it its modern name – one of which was found alongside those bianzhong bells in Yi's tomb.

In images from pharaonic Egypt (roughly 3000–300 BCE) we see musicians playing lutes and lyres, pipes of various sorts and percussion instruments, clapping, dancing and what looks like conducting with differing hand signals and shapes possibly indicating pitch. Egyptian music was connected with gods and goddesses, particularly the cow goddess Hathor – 'the lady of music' – who was credited with having brought music into the world. The sistrum, a metal rattle, is associated with her. It is clear that whatever might have happened among Egyptians of low rank, music was played by professionals in court and temple, with temple musicians, mostly women, at the top of the tree. If only we knew what music they played! The upper echelons of ancient Egyptian society were notably literate but, unlike their neighbours in Mesopotamia, they seem not to have written down their music.

Ancient Egyptian wall painting showing musicians

Of course, even if they had, it might not have helped us to gain a sense of how it sounded. When it comes to those clay tablets on which Mesopotamians notated music (see Chapter Two) we have little but conjecture to help us. However, no guesswork is required to say with confidence that the players of the lyres found at the royal burial grounds at Ur were women, because beside the lyres lay the bodies of the players, sacrificed together with other members of the royal household, and buried along with the king and queen. In one case the player's fingers were outstretched as though in the act of plucking the strings of her instrument.

In Mexico and Central America, royal tombs of the Mayan classical era (roughly 200 to 900 CE) are also troves of instruments – long trumpets made of clay and wood, and gourds, flutes, drums and large maracas. From surviving murals and painted vases, we know these instruments played in small orchestras of ten to twelve at important state occasions including religious sacrifices and in battle; they may even be seen accompanying the torture and sacrifice of captives. But music was particularly associated with gods and monarchs, as it was for the later Aztecs. It is no coincidence that the Spanish conquistadors often slaughtered Aztec musicians before anyone else and destroyed their instruments, considering them to be in the service of heathen gods.

Mayan vase depicting musicians accompanying torture

In much of the ancient world, music was evidently an important part of life in royal courts. It provided order, bolstered status, honoured gods and ancestors, but also provided entertainment. From the first millennium BCE, yǎyuè fulfilled these functions at the Chinese imperial court. The music was probably performed by a small orchestra of voices, wind and string instruments, slowly unspooling a melodic line in a ragged unison, punctuated by ritualised interjections from drums and other percussion instruments. As with most ancient music, it is difficult to make clear distinctions between what is folkloric and what is 'composed', and it seems likely that traditional forms and tunes were part of the makeup of yǎyuè. In addition to its role in court ceremonies, yǎyuè was also played in temples, and Confucius, who coined the term in his *Analects* ('yǎ – yuè' means 'elegant music'), stressed the moral benefits that flowed from music when correctly played.

* * *

> The Master said, 'I hate the manner in which purple takes away the lustre of vermilion. I hate the way in which the songs of zheng confound the music of the yǎ. I hate those who with their sharp mouths overthrow kingdoms and families.'
>
> —from the *Analects* of Confucius
> (c. 551 – c. 479 BCE)

The practice of yǎyuè died out in China, though tourists may be treated to speculative reconstructions, but in gagaku – the court music of Japan – we can perhaps hear something similar. The word 'gagaku' is the Japanese pronunciation of the Chinese characters for 'yǎyuè' (雅樂), but it seems unlikely that much of the yǎyuè repertoire made its way to Japan. From its beginnings in the early seventh century, the influences on gagaku included traditional songs from China and Korea. In 701, the first gagaku institute was established to perform and teach these sorts of music, for gagaku was never one thing. It was divided into indigenous and imported music, the latter eventually split into two main categories of pieces from Tang-dynasty China (tōgaku) and from Korea (komagaku).

Most of the world's notated music also involves aspects of an oral tradition in which memory plays a role, and gagaku is highly dependent on the players' memories. As is common throughout East and Southeast Asia, the teaching of a piece begins by singing, even if the music in question is purely instrumental. Teachers sing a melodic line and students repeat it. The melody must be memorised before any instruments are taken up.

Members of a gagaku orchestra

The most famous piece of gagaku is 'Etenraku' ('heavenly music'), famous in the West as well as in Japan, thanks to an orchestral arrangement popularised by the conductor Leopold Stokowski. Its origins are obscure, with most believing it to be Japanese in origin, others Chinese, while, somewhat fancifully, it has even been suggested the piece was composed by Han-dynasty Emperor Wen in the second century BCE. The stately theme consists of three thirty-two-beat phrases that are essentially variations on the one phrase, and they are usually played by an ensemble of instruments including the biwa (short-necked lute) and shō (mouth organ), the ryūteki (transverse bamboo flute) and the piercing, double-reed hichiriki, resembling a sawn-off oboe. The melody is performed heterophonously (the ragged unison mentioned above), the lines converging only on the regular slow beat of the taiko drum.

In the twelfth century, yǎyuè arrived at the Korean court (where the Chinese characters are pronounced 'aak') as a gift of hundreds of instruments and costumes from the Song-dynasty Emperor Huizong. The gift also included notated melodies, versions of which may still be heard in Korea today. But it is important to note that while these forms of orchestral court music – yǎyuè, gagaku and aak – share characteristics and some of the same compositions, other cultural influences affected the development of the music in each country. Not only were existing indigenous pieces absorbed into the new forms, but there were also influences from other cultures, among them India.

By the sixteenth century, yǎyuè had made its way to Vietnam. Here, the Chinese characters were pronounced 'nhã nhạc', and at the Đại Việt court, in what is modern Hanoi, the new music ran up against a number of existing styles. The kingdom of Champa in the south of modern Vietnam had for centuries traded in spices with China and Indonesia, Persia and India; accordingly, the Cham had a cosmopolitan outlook, and the Indian influence on their culture was particularly strong. Like the Balinese, the Cham were (basically) Hindu – and this was reflected in their music and dance, which must have seemed exotic in Buddhist Đại Việt. From the late tenth century, there were already Cham musicians at the Đại Việt court, but in 1044, the Emperor Lý Thái Tông invaded Champa, raiding its cities and capturing more singers and dancers, whom he housed in a specially built palace. Enslaved as they were, these women nevertheless had an honoured place at court, their music a diverting entertainment. Elements of their music in turn influenced nhã nhạc.

Along with musical compositions and styles, individual instruments also migrated. The koto and the shakuhachi, two instruments strongly associated with the music of Japan, both have their roots in China. The koto is a descendant of the zheng; the shakuhachi of the xiao. Both zheng and xiao were introduced to Japan in the seventh century.

A particularly vivid example of the migration of instruments is Madagascar's tube zither known as the valiha. Its name comes from the local bamboo used to make both its body and its strings (these days the strings are metal), and it is Madagascar's national instrument, but its design is based on a model taken to the island by Indonesian settlers who began to arrive about the sixth century. Tube zithers – where the instrument's neck is also its sound box – can also be found in Vietnam, Cambodia and the Philippines. By the nineteenth century, during the later period of the Merina Kingdom in

Madagascar, playing the valiha had become the preserve of the ruling Merina people, descendants of those who had brought the instrument to the island in the first place. Their aristocratic status was underlined by their long, zither-playing fingernails.

Sylvestre Randafison playing a valiha

As ubiquitous as the zither was the lute, an instrument found in varying forms throughout Asia, Africa and Europe, with either long necks or short. The short-necked version, which became common at European courts from the eleventh century and dominated Renaissance music, first arrived with Muslims in Spain and Sicily. The word 'lute', like the Arabic 'oud', is probably derived from 'al-'ūd', meaning wood, a reference, perhaps, to the instrument's wooden (as opposed to skin) soundboard.

Lutes with soundboards made of stretched skin have also existed since antiquity in Asia and Africa. The Japanese shamisen was a version of the Chinese sanxian, though an older Egyptian spiked lute, similar to the Persian tar, might have been the model for that. In the West, the banjo is the best-known example of this sort of instrument. It was developed in the seventeenth and eighteenth centuries by enslaved Africans on cotton, sugar or tobacco plantations in the southern United States, as well as in the Caribbean and among Creole communities in the northeastern part of South America, and it was

An akonting player in Guinea-Bissau

made of halved and hollowed gourds covered with goat or calf skin. Gourds and hide are a common combination in the making of instruments in Africa, particularly West Africa, and there are several possible prototypes there for the banjo. For example, the simbing and the kora, found in Gambia, Mali,

Senegal, Guinea and Guinea-Bissau, are halfway between a lute and a harp. The strings are connected to a bridge (as on a lute) and tied to the top of the long neck. But the neck is not a fingerboard, the pitches of the strings cannot be altered except by tuning, and the strings run vertically, like those of a harp. A closer relative of the banjo might be the akonting played by the Jola people of those same countries, which has two strings running up a fingerboard, plus a thumb string, and is held horizontally like a banjo.

* * *

> We wouldn't have the banjo without slavery. It wouldn't still be popular without minstrelsy.
>
> —Rhiannon Giddens (b. 1977), American singer, composer, banjo player

The banjo's story in the United States is fascinating and discomfiting, because after a century as a plantation instrument (along with the washboard and the washtub bass – both of which also have African roots), it found its way to minstrel shows where white musicians played it almost as a musical version of blackface. But if it was a novelty in minstrel shows, that didn't last. Instead, the banjo became the instrument of choice for singers in rural communities in the Appalachian Mountains, mostly descendants of immigrants from Ireland, Scotland and Wales, which is also where many of their songs originated. From there, it was a short step to the banjo's role as the archetypal sound of 1940s bluegrass – fast, flashy and overwhelmingly white. And yet, banjo playing persisted in African American communities, particularly in the Piedmont region east of the Appalachians, and some of those bluegrass finger patterns can be traced back to Africa.

It is probably true to say that West African rhythms and styles have had a greater effect on the world's music than those of any other region. The North American popular music forms that came to dominate the globe in the twentieth century and beyond – jazz, rock and roll and hip hop – could all trace at least some of their roots to West Africa. But the African influence went well beyond North America.

Approximately twelve million people were forcibly taken from Angola, the Congo, Benin, Nigeria, Sierra Leone and other West African regions between the sixteenth and nineteenth centuries – this number omits the millions who died on voyage or at 'seasoning camps', where the new arrivals were taken to get used to the climate, harsh treatment and malnutrition. Of the twelve million who made it, nearly half were enslaved in Portuguese Brazil. A similar number went to the Caribbean Islands colonised by the British, French and Spanish. Only just over 300,000 were taken to the United States – approximately 2.5 per cent.

African rhythms cross-pollinated with those of the coloniser and, in some cases, the indigenous peoples of a region, to create distinctive dance rhythms such as the Cuban rumba, mambo and son cubano, the Colombian cumbia and the Brazilian samba and jongo. Not that these dance forms and dozens of others remained fixed: they continue to change and adapt. In the case of the rumba, multiple varieties of which exist in Cuba alone, there is a wide range of offspring, some of which are rumba in name only; for instance, the so-called ballroom rhumba and the Congolese rumba that sprang up around Leopoldville (now Kinshasa) in the 1930s after recordings of son cubano were played on radio there.

While the rhythmic structures of dance might be the most pervasive vestiges of Africa in the music of Latin America and the Caribbean, they are not the only influences. In Trinidad and Tobago, for example, calypso can trace a direct line back to West Africa via kaiso music, a song form that often accompanied limbo dancing. Kaiso was further developed on sugar plantations by competing teams of slaves, who would challenge each other to stick fights. Each side's fighter was celebrated in song by a chantwell (*chantuelle*), a song leader whose verses were backed up by his fellow workers in a call-and-response manner. While talking up the chances of their man, the song heaped scorn on the opponent, and the lyrics were ribald and topical. In time the songs turned their focus on the authorities and these new songs frequently incorporated political commentary. The chantwells had become calypsonians.

It will be understood by now that most of the world's musical styles and forms are to some degree syncretic, and that instruments have travelled the globe. Perhaps the most common and least recognised repository of the world's instruments is the modern symphony orchestra, which developed in Europe during the eighteenth and nineteenth centuries.

Many of its instruments have ancient precursors, some from outside Europe. This is particularly true of the percussion section, which grew into its present form during the twentieth century.

Most of the percussion instruments in the symphony orchestra had already travelled across centuries and cultures before the orchestra adopted them. Kettle drums, for instance, usually called timpani in an orchestra, seem to have originated in Persia and Mesopotamia, then spread to Africa and beyond; cymbals, which are older, also have Middle Eastern origins, though they were in China and eastern Europe by the twelfth century; tambourines are frame drums (again Middle Eastern and older still) with jingles attached. Gongs are Asian: the word 'gong' is Javanese, and gongs of various sorts dominate the percussion orchestras of Java and Bali, Thailand, Myanmar and the southern Philippines, Borneo, eastern Indonesia and East Timor. But the oldest gongs are Chinese, and by the first century they were already in the Roman Empire. Xylophones form part of all those Southeast Asian percussion orchestras, but they are widespread in sub-Saharan Africa, and it is hard to say which came first, or even if they are related. The African instruments often have gourd resonators, and this is especially true of the larger, deeper marimba, taken to South America in the sixteenth century by African slaves. All these and other percussion instruments now commonly make up the 'back row' of a symphony orchestra, and yet, unlike the longer-established wind, brass and string instruments, they are still sometimes thought of as 'exotic'.

There may be several reasons for this. One, which is purely musical, is that the core repertoire of symphony orchestras is historical (music from the mid-eighteenth to mid-twentieth centuries) and almost exclusively harmonic; it is music in which pitch is of primary importance and the combining of pitches into chords and keys forms the music's organising principle. Percussion instruments might add colour and emphasis, but they contributed little from a harmonic point of view. It took a twentieth-century crisis in Western harmony (see Chapter Four) before percussion instruments gained something like parity with the other sections of the orchestra, and percussion ensembles in their own right began to appear. But in Asia and Africa, where music is melodic, rhythmic and timbral, percussion instruments have been vital since prehistory. What's more, the gestural nature of percussion playing suits ritual: you can see the action of a gong being struck in a way that you can't see breath going into a flute, and ritual depends upon precise, repeated action. Accordingly, percussion instruments – particularly gongs and drums – have been and remain participants in religious and state ritual throughout Asia and Africa.

In the central African region of Burundi, for example, drums, ritual and law-making went hand in hand for hundreds of years. The drum was a symbol of the monarch, and drummers formed a part of the king's retinue, the word 'ingoma' meaning both drum and kingdom in the Kirundi language. After the abolition of the monarchy in 1966, the distinctive synchronised drumming that we hear today when the Royal Drummers of Burundi perform became something of a national pastime, with women taking part in the traditionally patrilineal pursuit. But as recently as 2017 the Burundian president outlawed women's participation and restricted performances to formal occasions, in the interests of 'preserving and protecting tradition.

Among the Lozi, who live along the floodplains of the Zambezi, royal music is characterised by singing in an ancient language that is not part of daily life, while royal percussionists play small, portable xylophones and drums. The national drum, large and painted, is the maoma, its beating alerting the Lozi to the rising of the water levels and warning them to move to higher ground. This ritual is known as the kuomboka, and the maoma travels with the king in his royal barge. Only men may play this drum.

* * *

> Songspirals connect us through the generations,
> to our knowledge, to those that have come before
> and those yet to emerge.
>
> —from *Songspirals* by the Gay'wu Group of Women

In discussing the ritual uses of music, it is important to emphasise that this term 'music' is problematic. The Buddhist priest striking a gong does not consider it a musical act, and neither does the Lozi man playing the maoma. Both, indeed, are probably closer to the Yolŋu notion of song as knowledge, the passing on of this knowledge vital to the health of the culture. Songs, of course, contain words as well as music, but it would no more occur to most traditional societies to distinguish between these elements than it would to listeners of modern pop music. A song is a song.

Poetry uses words in a musical manner. For this reason there has been confusion throughout history and across cultures about where poetry ends and music begins. The ancient Chinese *Shijing* – variously known as 'The Classic of Poetry' or 'The Book of Odes' – consists of the words (and only the words) of Han-dynasty folk songs, meant to be declaimed if not sung. Five hundred years before that, Homer's *Odyssey* seems to have been recited to a musical accompaniment, a strummed lyre at least, and so does the Anglo-Saxon epic *Beowulf* – indeed, we might surmise that this is true of most ancient Greek and Anglo-Saxon poetry. The Indian epics, the *Ramayana* and the *Mahābhārata*, were chanted, and still are. In the griot tradition of West Africa, the hereditary bards were as much singers as poets, many also players of the kora, and their modern descendants may be thought of as singer–songwriters.

The thirteenth-century Persian poet Rūmī played the rebab – a two-stringed fiddle – believing its sound the gateway to enlightenment; did he also accompany his poems? A century later, Ḥāfeẓ, building on Rūmī's example, embraced the song-like ghazal form and his words were rapidly taken up by Persian musicians. Did he intend this? Did he imagine his words sung? Did he sing them himself? We know from his contemporaries that the English poet William

Blake (1757–1827) sang his poems, some of which were called songs ('of Innocence and of Experience'). But what tunes did he sing them to? Were they self-composed or off-the-peg? If the latter, did he sometimes write his words to fit well-known tunes? This was still a common enough practice in the London of Blake's childhood, where broadside ballads recounting murders and executions were sold without music, but with a suggested tune that would fit the words; and it is precisely how Blake's contemporaries, the Scot Robert Burns (1759–1796) and the Irishman Thomas Moore (1779–1852), composed much of their poetry.

Rap evolved in 1970s New York out of an MC's improvised banter spoken over the looped drum breaks of soul and funk records into an art form all its own, the rhymes and rhythms of speech creating the principal musical interest. The instrumental backing to many of the earliest examples of rap used just a limited melodic/harmonic template in order to focus on the rapper's voice. In 1979 this was apparently still such a surprising development that the Sugarhill Gang's 'Rapper's Delight' reassured its listeners that what they were hearing was 'not a test' but an actual record. In short order, rappers such as Tupac Shakur, Snoop Dogg and Eminem were among the biggest names in music. The opening words of 'Rapper's Delight' had been 'hip hop', and by the end of the twentieth century hip hop had become the world's dominant musical culture. It seemed rap could adjust to any language, subtly transforming itself as it met the guttural consonants of Arabic, the strongly rolled *r*s and front-loaded word stresses of Finnish or the tonal inflections of Mandarin, the last of which created a palette of vocal timbre and pitch somewhat at odds with the comparatively monotonous delivery typical of Western rap.

So, music and words not only colour each other's meaning, but words may become music. This symbiotic relationship has played a significant role in all the world's great religions, although the nature of the music itself is often theologically controversial. There are two broad strands of sacred music, one designed to resemble or induce religious ecstasy, the other where the music is predominantly the bearer of text. The aim of the latter is generally doctrinal. Words are more memorable if they are chanted, the heightening of the musical elements of speech – pitch, rhythm, tempo, dynamics and timbre – conveying a religious message or any other message (political slogans, multiplication tables) more powerfully than had the words been simply spoken or read off the page. But here is the point of controversy, for is this music? Is it even singing?

The English word 'chant' comes from the French word to sing, so there is a clear connection. Yet while most people would agree that Christian plainsong – notated and sung in European monasteries since the early medieval period – is indeed song, we know that it developed from something that was merely song-*like*, early chant notation indicating the rising and falling of tone, but no specific indication of pitch. And while Hinduism's Vedic tradition, Hebrew chant and the recitation of the Qur'ān involve similar musical components – as we've seen, even naturalistic speech has music in it – most Hindus, Jews and Muslims would insist there is a difference. It's a difference of intent, and it stems from the suspicion that music is frivolous (Steven Pinker would agree) and a distraction – maybe even a seduction.

* * *

> Samā is the soul's adornment helping it
> to discover love, to feel the shudder of the
> encounter, to remove the veils and be in
> God's presence.
>
> —Jalāl ad-Dīn Muḥammad Rūmī (1207–1273),
> Persian poet

By the time Rūmī wrote those words, Islamic scholars had already spent half a millennium debating the permissibility of music, and Rūmī, in encapsulating the argument in its favour, also draws our attention to the dangers by dwelling on the physical responses that music can provoke. The Qur'ān is silent on the matter, but many Muslims consider instrumental music – if not all music – forbidden and refuse to countenance the possibility that chanting of a sacred text is related to music on any level. To certain Sufi orders, however, the practice of samā or deep listening is central to the 'remembrance of God'.

Sufism began in ninth- or tenth-century Baghdad and is best thought of as Islamic mysticism. Not all Sufis embrace the practice of samā, but the most famous order does so in spectacular fashion. This is the Mevlevi order, founded by

Rūmī and his followers in Turkey and popularly known as the whirling dervishes. Both the whirling and the music, which often involves singers as well as instruments (typically the ney – a long, thin, end-blown flute – and percussion), start out in a stately manner, but as the ceremony continues both tend to speed up. In the ecstasy (wajd) induced by their whirling, the dervishes 'burn' their egos, drawing closer to God.

Among the Sufi fundamentalists who disapprove of the Mevlevis' whirling is the Chishti order, which originated in Afghanistan and today is found mostly there and on the Indian subcontinent. Yet while they may frown on the whirling, Chishtis have their own path to ecstasy in song form, qawwali, developed by the Sufi saint Amīr Khusrau, a contemporary of Rūmī. Qawwali draws on the ragas of the classical Hindustani tradition for its scales and structure, a slow, exploratory introduction leading to a steady rhythm and melody, then faster and faster with much spontaneous ornamentation. Originally, instruments were banned, but the drone necessary to the performance of a raga had to come from somewhere, and so did the important rhythmic component. By the late twentieth century, the Pakistani singer Nusrat Fateh Ali Khan had transformed qawwali into something that could be performed at outdoor music festivals around the world in epic performances, his voice wheeling and flying ever higher, ever faster in a spiritual ecstasy that communicated itself to listeners who understood not a word he was singing.

As with the classical raga, the performance of qawwali involves considerable improvisation, often with nonsense syllables, not unlike scat singing in jazz. It is another example of verbal sounds turning into music. Hindu and Buddhist mantras are similar; Pentecostal Christians speak in tongues: in each case the believer is aiming to forget the self, to draw closer to God or, to use the Muslim expression, to the 'remembrance of God', and it reminds us that even at its most communal, the religious experience is intensely personal, the paradox being that its goal is the elimination of the self. But this is also the musical experience, which is why music is central to branches of so many religions and why it is perceived as a threat by others.

* * *

> The baby is soothed by lullabies and lays
>   aside his burden;
> He listens silently to the one who soothes him,
> Her sweet song making him forget his
>   bitter state
> And remember a secret whisper of
>   ancient times.
>
> —from *The Poem of the Sufi Way,*
> Ibn al-Farid (1181–1234), Arab poet

Ibn al-Farid was writing in the thirteenth century about how music and the deep listening of samā release the mind and body from quotidian worries, allowing unfettered contemplation of the divine. But what he says in those lines about lullabies is in some ways central to this history of music. He reminds us, for one thing, that while the performance of music may occur in courts and temples, in concert halls and at outdoor festivals, the *ur*-performance takes place at the end of our childhood bed. It happens before we are able to understand words; we are soothed and reassured by the sound of a parent's voice. It is music at its most domestic and least self-conscious, because it is music that embodies ritual and function. It is ritualistic, in that it happens every night and works best when it happens in the same way – the parent who introduces new repertoire will almost certainly be met with resistance. It is functional, because it is a work song. The lullaby conveys love – that is part of its purpose – but its main job is to get a child to sleep.

* * *

I heard the songs:
the thunder songs,
the dancing songs,
the fire-starting songs,
the day-break songs,
the flute songs
for the grinding of corn.
—Corn-grinding song, trad. Pueblo Indian

Work songs exist in all cultures – there is evidence of them in ancient Egypt and Mesopotamia – and they fall broadly into two categories. There are songs about work, with lyrics cursing the luck of the worker, and songs sung during work itself, the rhythm and structure of which help get the work done. Most lullabies are in a 6/8 metre (two big beats, each consisting of three smaller beats), mimicking the rocking of a cradle. The maritime version of the work song was the shanty, sung aboard ships to assist with hauling sails and anchors, again with a rhythm suited to the work. Call and response is a common feature of songs sung on the job, and nineteenth-century merchant ships would often employ a shantyman, a sort of musical foreman, to lead the crew in shanty singing. He would strike up the shanty appropriate to short-haul, halyard or windlass work, the last requiring synchronised footsteps, the other sailors joining in on certain lines.

In the eighteenth and nineteenth centuries in the southern United States, call-and-response field hollers or 'arhoolies' had a similar function among enslaved workers on plantations. The practice carried over to chain gangs, lasting well into the twentieth century, with picks and hoes creating a percussive pulse to the back-breaking work. In the United States armed forces, cadence calls are another example of the work song, this time for marching and running. Though distinct from each other, such hollers and calls, from the plantation to the parade ground, share blue notes – fully or microtonally flattened thirds, fifths and sevenths – that, like the proto-banjo, originated in West Africa. They also share a world-turned-upside-down quality, in which things that could never be said out loud may be sung out loud, as Trinidadian calypso singers do. Bosses – slave owners, prison guards, drill sergeants – come in for abuse, sometimes disguised, as did ships' captains in shanties. For that matter, in lullabies, even the baby (who fortunately can't understand the words) can find itself the subject of sweetly delivered threats and admonishments: 'When the bough breaks the cradle will fall / Down will come baby, cradle and all'. Lullabies are as much for the parent as for the child.

* * *

> I would venture to guess that Anon, who wrote
> so many poems without signing them, was
> often a woman.
>
> —from *A Room of One's Own*,
> Virginia Woolf (1882–1941), English novelist

Notwithstanding the use of various forms of notation in Mesopotamia and China, in gagaku and aak, all the music discussed in this chapter belongs to oral traditions, which exist in every culture and not only in relation to music. Predating mass communication and recording, these songs, rhymes and stories were only written down after they had existed for decades if not centuries, and for that reason they were mostly unattributed. What today we call 'folk songs' are repositories of history, but also of emotion; of intrigue and adventure and derring-do, but also of love and family. The domestic nature of their storytelling might well be thought to support Virginia Woolf's theory of anonymity, but it would be a mistake to regard the songs as cosy and reassuring.

In 2023, a publisher's puff for a book by a pop psychologist told its readers to expect a 'journey from the wasteland of modern society to a place of nourishment and connection', and that's how folk songs can sometimes seem to modern listeners: they take us back to a pre-industrial time when all went well. Yet such sentimentalised readings of traditional songs are only possible if one disregards the endemic violence and great sadness depicted in so many of them.

There is also a wider danger associated with looking at the culture of traditional societies. All over the world, traditional forms of music, which may be hundreds of years old, continue today. In other places, they have died out completely, often as a result of colonisation, or they have become endangered. In New Zealand, a last-ditch salvage operation has helped to revive interest in taonga pūoro, the traditional instruments of the Māori people, and to return the instruments to use. But whether we are looking at continuing traditions or those that have been preserved or revived, the danger is in assuming that the traditions never changed; that the rhymes and stories, the tunes and dances we encounter today are exactly as they were when first invented; that by singing the songs and dancing the dances we are tapping the source and returning to that 'place of nourishment and connection'.

Why should oral traditions remain unchanged? We know that traditional instruments have changed because we can see examples. The British Museum has a didgeridoo collected in Australia's Northern Territory in the 1840s. It is made of cane and is the size and shape of a medium-sized shakuhachi or tenor recorder, less than a metre long and just over three centimetres in diameter. It is no one's idea of a didgeridoo in the twenty-first century.

An object such as a didgeridoo might change its design because someone thought it could be improved, but traditional music is dependent upon memory, and memory is so often a matter of human frailty. Songs are passed from singer to singer and the aim will be to convey them precisely and remember them exactly. In most Westernised cultures, oral traditions are less important today than they once were, but jokes are a small example of how oral traditions work. If you have been told a joke that made you laugh, you may wish to tell others, and you will make an effort to get it right, to repeat it as exactly as possible. If you forget a line, the joke may no longer seem funny. Few of us, however, are possessed of perfect memories, and so we adapt the joke in order to retell it to the best of our ability.

Among the traditional songs in the British Isles, we find certain ballads that exist in dozens of different versions from Scotland to the southwest of England. Some of these songs crossed the Atlantic Ocean to fetch up in the Appalachian Mountains; some were in Scandinavia before they were in Scotland or England or Ireland. A song might tell the same story, and individual lines will be the same, but, over centuries of telling, key details will change, including names and genders. Tunes are similarly transformed; and tunes and words become separated, particularly when a version of the words is written down without its music. There are also common pools of phrases, verbal and musical, that crop up in song after song, familiar tropes – clichés, if you will – that are perhaps substituted for forgotten or misheard or misremembered lines and phrases. They are everywhere in orally transmitted songs and stories: consider only the number of blues songs that have as their opening line a version of 'I woke up this morning' or the traditional English songs that begin 'As I walked out'.

* * *

> I regard tradition as progressive, and a traditional song as a progressive force because it is concerned with the continuity of things.
>
> —Martin Carthy (b. 1941), English folk singer

Oral traditions were sidelined by industrialised societies. Traditional culture was 'collected', written down, published in books and then, in many cases, shelved and forgotten. But just as one may find derelict industrial sites where nature is reclaiming its land, so oral traditions will sometimes appropriate composed music and literature. Lines from poetry enter everyday speech – Shakespeare's plays are the most bountiful sources in the English language – and musical phrases creep in from classical music. Take the Western world's most famous wedding music. Everyone can hum the bridal march ('Here Comes the Bride'), but how many people know that it comes from Richard Wagner's opera *Lohengrin*?

And the fanfare-encrusted march with which the organist sends the newlyweds out of the church? It's from Felix Mendelssohn's incidental music for Shakespeare's *A Midsummer Night's Dream*. Staying with marches, the funeral march that most people would know is by Frédéric Chopin, the slow movement of his second piano sonata. These familiar bits of music are now part of a contemporary oral tradition in which their composers are as anonymous as the creators of nursery rhymes and the first knock-knock joke.

And what of ages-old traditional music? Perhaps it was always endangered. For traditional music to continue (as traditions must or they are no longer traditions), it has to be passed on and used by new generations. But keeping tradition alive requires dedication, and old people have always looked at young people and wondered if they had enough of that. When Frank Kidson published *Traditional Tunes* in 1891, bringing together songs collected in the British Isles, he wrote in his introduction that this sort of song 'is fast disappearing before the modern productions, and any young ploughboy who should sing the songs his father or grandfather sung, would be laughed to scorn'.

This is the perennial worry of traditional societies: that young people won't remember, or will lack the nerve to continue singing and to pass it on. The Gay'wu Women's Group lament the fact that many younger Yolŋu women 'don't join in' with milkarri.

'We are frightened it will stop,' they say, 'there will be no voices. Sometimes we think we'll go to our graves not explaining lots of things – it will be lost. Already, there have been some songspirals destroyed. There are only a few people who know how to sing milkarri. The worry is the women of our age, the middle-aged ladies, not joining in. Maybe they are shy.'

2

MUSIC AND NOTATION: BLUEPRINTS FOR BUILDING IN SOUND FROM 1400 BCE TO THE PRESENT

FORTY SINGERS STAND BEFORE US in a semicircle, eight little choirs, each of five voices – soprano, alto, tenor, baritone and bass. The soprano on our extreme left begins to sing in Latin, but before she reaches the end of her first word, another voice joins in, then another and another and another. The music, building in complexity, crosses the semicircle from left to right like a slow Mexican wave, the first singers gradually dropping out as new singers take over. When the last singers have joined in, all the others return: forty voices singing at once. Now the wave goes into reverse, the music passing back from right to left until, again, all the voices join in. Then suddenly there's silence. It's only a split second, but in the context of the dense web of polyphony we've just experienced, it is a striking moment. Having sung first as eight choirs of five voices, then as a single choir of forty, the singers now divide themselves into four choirs of ten voices, bouncing musical ideas back and forth before a final section of glorious forty-part counterpoint in the new key of A major (up to this point the music had been in C). This is *Spem in alium*, composed sometime before 1570 by the Tudor composer Thomas Tallis, and he couldn't have done it without manuscript paper and a pen.

* * *

> A verbal art like poetry is reflective; it stops to think. Music is immediate; it goes on to become.
>
> —W.H. Auden (1907–1973), English poet

Musical sounds exist in time and the time is always now. It doesn't matter whether the music is spontaneously improvised, remembered from childhood or sung from a 500-year-old manuscript: it is made in the present. The manuscript is a repository of music, but it is not the thing itself. For any music fully to exist, it must be lifted off the page and played or sung. In that moment – in the here and now – it comes to life.

Modern notation had its origins in eleventh-century Europe. Much developed and refined, it led to the composition and preservation of the world's largest body of music, loosely called 'classical music', somewhat (though only somewhat) more accurately known as Western art music. But in the eleventh century, music notation had already existed elsewhere for more than two millennia.

Why do we write music down? Why do we write anything

down? In the first place, to remember it. Just as we might make a packing list so we don't forget things, we jot down a tune so we can sing it again in more or less the same way. Until the invention of sound recording, there was no means of preserving music except by trying to remember it. But what was being preserved in the earliest forms of notation? Lists of instruments, information about tuning strings and instructions for playing and singing the music itself: it's a tantalising glimpse of something we can never hear, because even if we could fully understand the instructions, the instruments no longer exist.

The earliest example of notated music is the cuneiform writing on baked clay tablets in the city of Ugarit in what is now Syria, dating from around 1400 BCE. The notation evidently relates to a set of approximately thirty-six hymns (because they are in fragments, it is hard to be certain of the number). They're known as the Hurrian Hymns, after the Hurrian people and their language, and one of them – the Hymn to Nikkal, a goddess of orchards – has a complete set of lyrics and some instructions for accompanying the singing on a lyre.

Among the many problems faced when attempting to decipher the notation is that we don't understand Hurrian very well. Also, it is hard to be sure of the relationship between the words and the music, because interpreting the music itself is largely a matter of conjecture. It is clear from one tablet that the lyre has nine strings, and we know something about their tuning and the intervals between the strings. But there is no real indication of melody or rhythm. Consequently, every modern attempt to produce a reading of the Hurrian Hymn to Nikkal – and there have been quite a few – has resulted in a substantially different piece of music.

Many of the Sanskrit hymns in the Hindu *Rig Veda* date from around this same period, so when they were written down, probably in the third century BCE, they had already been chanted for a thousand years. The chanting, known as samagan, consisted initially of three tones or tonal accents derived from the pitch accents of Sanskrit. They were later expanded to seven accents and eventually resulted in the ragas of Indian classical music. Since the Sanskrit texts were annotated with these accents, the *Rig Veda* itself offered a musical

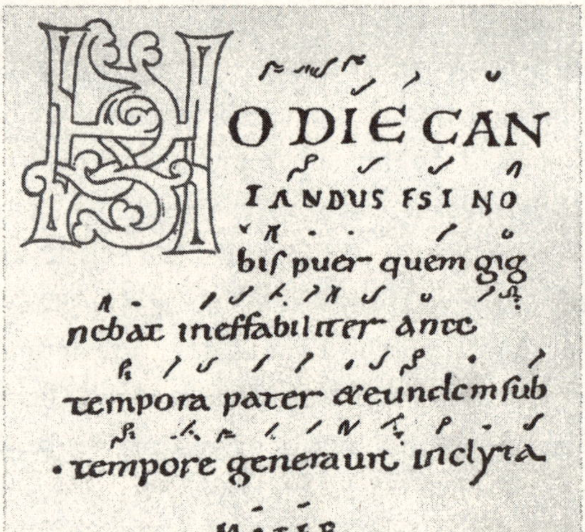

Plainsong in neume notation

score of sorts, similar to those of Greek and Byzantine chant and early Western plainsong, in which neumes placed above the words indicated the rising and falling of pitches without being precise about them. This sort of notation was really an aide-mémoire. If you knew or half remembered the melodic contour to which you had previously sung the words, the neumes might help you sing them again, but you couldn't pick up one of these scores and sightread it. Also, this was music for a single voice or voices singing in unison. Anything more elaborate was going to require a system of notation capable of providing specific information about pitch.

The naming of notes, known as solmisation, began, one may assume, with the naming of tonal accents in speech. Many musical cultures use a system of solmisation. The version most familiar to Western musicians is solfège, probably invented by an Italian monk, Guido of Arezzo, in the eleventh century. He called the notes Ut, Re, Mi, Fa, Sol and La, taking their names from an acrostic of an eighth-century hymn to John the Baptist in which each line began a step (or half a step) higher than the last: *Ut queant laxis / Resonare fibris / Mira gestorum / Famuli tuorum / Solve polluti / Labii reatum / Sancte Iohannes*. The so-called Guidonian Hand was invented, employing the fingers and their joints as a mnemonic technique.

Fans of Rodgers and Hammerstein will notice that Do and Ti are missing from Guido's scale. The more singable Do replaced Ut in the sixteenth century, but it wasn't until the eighteenth that Si was added – formed from the initials of Sancte Iohannes (Saint John). Until then, if you wanted to go beyond six notes, you had to rename La as Mi and start all over, a cumbersome way of doing things. The addition of Si solved that. (In the

English-speaking world, Si finally became Ti in the nineteenth century, paving the way for Julie Andrews.)

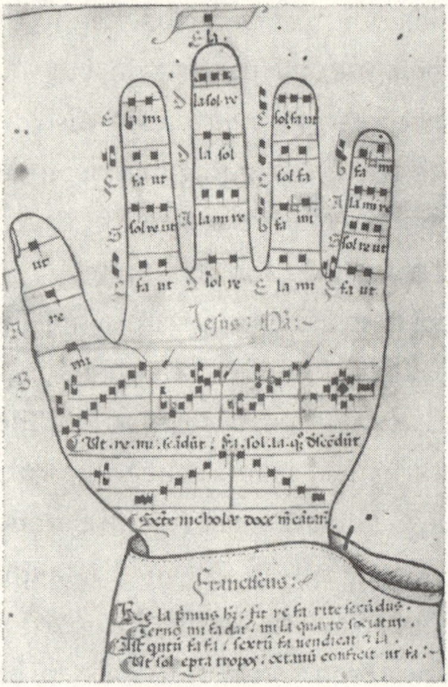

Guidonian Hand

But even with the seven-note scale (that will bring us back to Do), there are still limitations with solfège and two distinct ways of applying it. In one version, Do is the note C, Re is D, Mi is E and so on, and they never change. But there is also the concept of the movable Do, in which Do becomes the first note of whatever scale you happen to be dealing with. Either way, it is clear that solfège and its equivalent systems are a formalisation of the oral transmission of music. In classical Indian music, sargam – Sa, Re, Ga, Ma, Pa, Dha and Ni – is used by teachers to pass on ragas to their students, and sometimes by a performer wanting to call out to an audience the details of a raga.

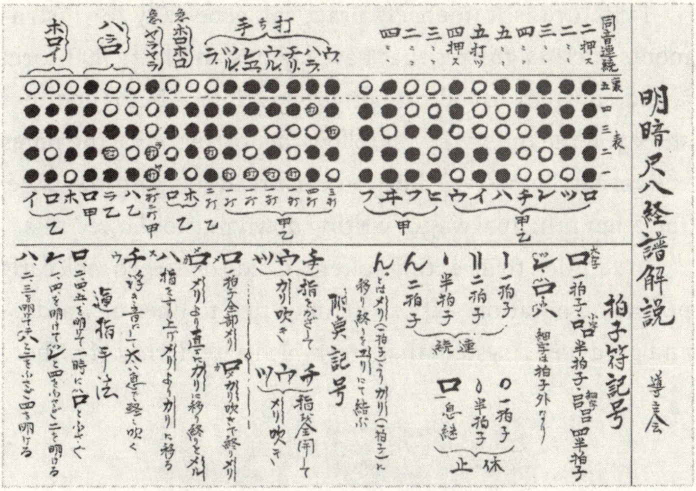

An example of shakuhachi notation

To move beyond being a teaching tool or a vehicle for virtuoso vocalising, solmisation needed a visual form more advanced than the Guidonian Hand. Two principal systems of notation evolved. One was tablature, which guitarists and ukulele players will immediately recognise as the notation that tells them where to place their fingers on a fretboard. This kind of notation was used for the Chinese guqin as early as the sixth century, employing words and, later, symbols to communicate the hand positions. Another version of this was – and still is – used in Japan for the notation of shakuhachi music. European examples include organ tablature dating from medieval times, while from the fifteenth century tablature was used for the lute and the Spanish vihuela (an instrument tuned like a lute but resembling a small guitar).

Tablature is immensely practical, especially for instruments such as guitars that have strings and frets that form a grid on which to indicate finger positions – but it does not show you the music. If you follow the instructions, the notes will reveal themselves, but you can't read them off the page. The other principal way of writing down music allowed this.

In addition to inventing solfège, Guido of Arezzo took early plainsong notation – those neumes tied to lines of words – and produced a system that resembled a modern score. There

A gradual, c. 1469.

were four-line staves or staffs instead of the familiar five lines, and the notation of rhythm was primitive: there were no dynamics or articulation markings or tempo indications. But we look at these manuscripts and recognise them as sheet music. Rather than telling you where and how to place your fingers on an instrument, the notation shows the desired outcome; it is a representation of the music itself.

Guido's notation was intended for voices more than instruments, but it was also for composers. Because they could now see as well as hear their music, it became easier to strategise, to use the staves as a means of working out complex combinations of pitches and rhythms and pitting voices against each other. A composer might, for example, arrange to have a musical line sung backwards, a tricky if not impossible feat by ear alone, and this is precisely what the medieval French composer Guillaume de Machaut (c. 1300–1377) did in his rondeau 'Ma fin est mon commencement' ('My end is my beginning'). There are three voices in the song, the top two of which have identical lines of music except that the second voice has the top line back-to-front. The third voice has a line that is its own mirror image, turning back on itself from the middle and ending where it had started. In other words, the song is one big palindrome. It is important to stress that Machaut's conceit in this piece is, to all intents and purposes, inaudible. Because the third part contains its own palindrome, that singer might spot what is going on, but the performers of the top two lines wouldn't necessarily be aware at all, since in the fourteenth century singers didn't have full scores containing all the parts of a piece but sang from single lines of music showing their individual parts. 'Ma fin est mon commencement' is a musical game, and armed with notation as a compositional aid, Western composers would never tire of playing these sorts of games.

There is game-playing aplenty in Tallis's *Spem in alium*, composed two hundred years after Machaut's rondeau in the England of Elizabeth I. It is possible the piece was the result of a wager, after Thomas Howard, the Duke of Norfolk, wondered aloud why no English composer had yet written anything comparable to the Italian Alessandro Striggio's forty-part choral works recently heard in London. Another explanation for the scope of Tallis's motet is that he wanted to celebrate the impending birthday of his queen and patron, who was about to turn forty. Whatever prompted him to work on such a scale, the composer adapted the structure to fit his text.

Musical word-painting in European music dates back at least to the twelfth century, when Hildegard of Bingen created startlingly precise illustrations of burgeoning nature or the voices of angels using melody alone, a single line seeming to wind around itself or reach for heaven. But during the late fifteenth and sixteenth centuries, this practice reached new levels of sophistication.

Tallis's Latin text, adapted from the Book of Judith, begins, 'I have never put my hope in any but you, God of Israel', and it is significant that his setting should start with a single voice that quickly becomes two, proliferating into five, then ten, then twenty voices, the individual believer turning into a congregation of the faithful before our very ears. At the end, that falling modulation from C to A matches the final words of the motet addressed to God: '*Respice humilitatem nostram*' – 'Look upon our lowliness'. For the listener, the architecture of the piece is no less overwhelming than the resultant wall of sound (the key change may signal humility, but the sonority is triumphant); from the singer's point of view, the experience is one of interdependence. Each of the forty performers has a unique part to sing, yet the individual lines continually join up with each other, making an evolving web of pitch connections. So at one point Alto 12 (that is, the alto in the third quintet) is singing the same note as Alto 17 (in the fourth quintet), before joining up with Tenor 38, then Tenor 28, then Tenor 18, then Baritone 24. All this occurs within a ten-second span of music, the singers continually aware of their melodic lines momentarily touching those of others. Neither Tallis's grand design for *Spem in alium* nor its intricate internal structure would have been possible without notation.

* * *

> There's music in all things, if men had ears;
> The earth is but the music of the spheres.
>
> —from *Don Juan* by
> Lord Byron (1788–1824), English poet

Before going further, it will be necessary to get technical for a page or two more. In Chapter One there were references to the harmonic series and to a diatonic scale. It's time to explain what these are and a couple of other things besides.

The harmonic series comes down to physics. In a way, all music does. Take a length of string – a guitar or cello string would be perfect, but really any string will do. When it is stretched tight and plucked, it will give you a pitch. We can call this pitch the fundamental and it's a complex thing, for in addition to the pitch that you can clearly hear, the fundamental contains a series of overtones or harmonics. You can reveal the first overtone by plucking the string while lightly touching it at its halfway point. This overtone will sound one octave higher than the fundamental, so if the plucked string originally gave you the fundamental C, this first overtone will be the C above it.

Example 1

If, instead of touching the string at its halfway point, you touch it a third of the way along, you will find the next overtone, which is G a fifth higher than the first overtone. The next overtone (at the quarter) will give C again (higher still), the next E, then another G, then something like B flat, and so on. As the divisions of the string get smaller, the overtones become higher and the intervals between them narrower. The same is true with any fundamental, and it applies not only to tightly stretched strings but also to columns of air, ranging from beer bottles to organ pipes to French horns.

Take the overtone C an octave above the fundamental, and the next G a fifth higher, and continue that pattern going up a fifth each time from G to D, D to A, A to E, E to B, and then bring those notes into the same octave: you will have a pentatonic (five-note) scale that is the basis of nearly all the music discussed in Chapter One. Depending upon the starting note, the scale will have a different distribution of intervals between the notes.

Pentatonic scale

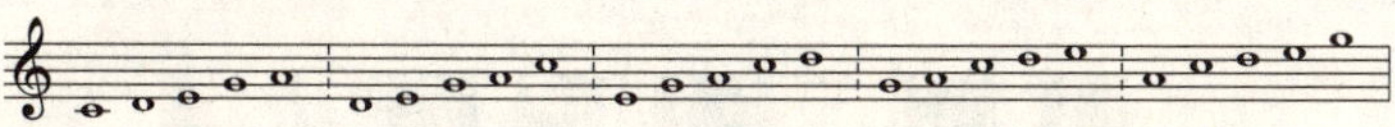

Example 2

Continue that pattern of ascending fifths, and you will uncover the chromatic scale – all twelve pitches on the piano, black and white.

Chromatic scale

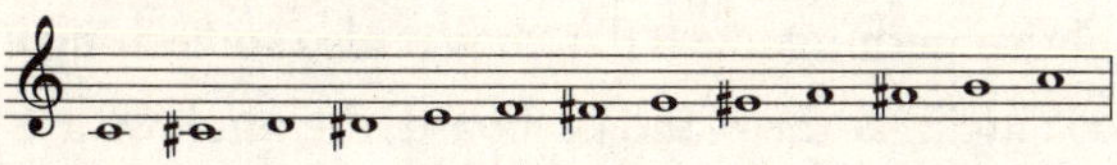

Example 3

Finally, fill out the octave C to C with just the white notes – C, D, E, F, G, A, B – and you will have a diatonic scale, made up of whole tones and semitones, with C as the home or tonic.

Diatonic scale (C major)

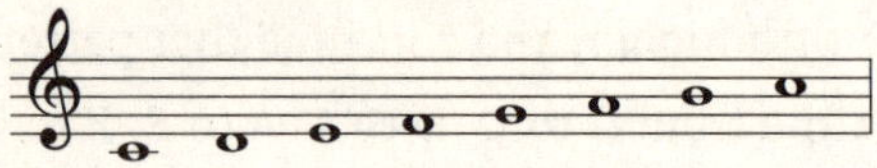

Example 4

This is Do Re Mi, etc. (A whole tone is an interval of two steps on the keyboard – say from C to D, jumping over the black note C sharp; a semitone is two adjacent notes, say E to F, where no black key intervenes.)

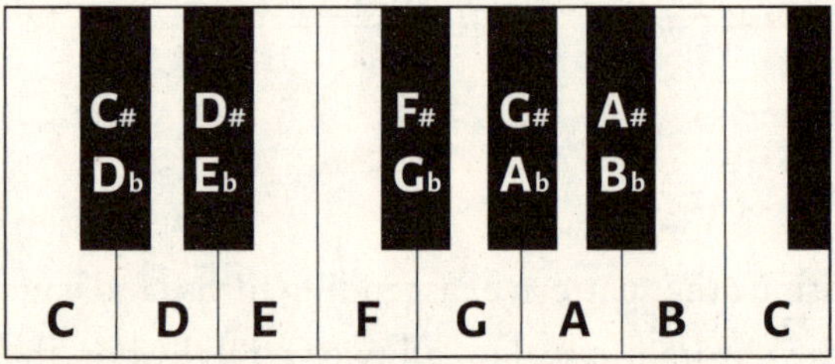

But there is an important piece of information missing. Remember, earlier, that the sixth overtone of C wasn't B flat, but only 'something like B flat'. It was also something like A. If you look again at the piano keyboard, the pitch we are talking about isn't there. It's in the crack between A and B flat. This is because pianos are not tuned to the harmonic series – if they were, their keyboards would be immensely long – but to a compromise. Natural tuning, based on the harmonic series, is considerably more complex than the tuning of a piano keyboard because nature doesn't compromise. To ears used to equal temperament, that 'A/B flat' will sound out of tune, and so will some of the other harmonics going up the series. These 'out-of-tune' harmonics are indicated with arrows in Example 1 on page 58.

As mentioned, pentatonic scales are not limited to one sort. Depending which notes the scales start on, they can have quite different characteristics because of the distribution of the intervals between the notes. It's the same with diatonic scales. The ancient Greek modes (scales) are a good example of this, complex and subtle things with long and convoluted histories that do not deserve to be reduced to 'happy' and 'sad', but nonetheless came to be thought of that way, just as, later and with even less justification, did major and minor scales. So the so-called Dorian mode is dark while the Lydian is bright; the Ionian is a sunny mode, but the Phrygian somehow gloomy.

While the internal ordering of whole tones and semitones accounts for most of the differences between these scales, natural tuning also plays a part. On a piano keyboard, C sharp and D flat are the same note. In nature, they are different notes, the sharp a bit flatter, the flat a bit sharper. For this reason, the scales that form the bases of Arabic maqams, Persian dastgahs and Indian ragas are all more than just rows of pitches. Each maqam, each dastgah, each raga has individual characteristics similar to those of the Greek modes, suggestive of certain melodic approaches. In the North Indian tradition, ragas are so distinct from each other and so much a part of Hindustani culture that they are associated with different times of day; no musician would play a morning raga in the evening or an afternoon raga just before dawn.

The distinguishing features of Greek, Arabic, Persian and Indian music are melody, rhythm and, in many cases, timbre. The same may generally be said of the traditional musics of Asia and Africa, America and Australia. Whether or not the music is vocal, all these melodic forms are linked to song; all involve improvisation to some extent; and all have a drone, real or implied. Most of these musical traditions underpin melodic invention with a distinctive rhythmic framework. Yet to say that such music is not harmonic is only partly true.

Harmony is generated by combining two or more pitches, but even in an unaccompanied melody there can be harmonic tension. Whether or not there is a sounding drone – but especially if there is – the notes of the melodic line can tug at the tonic note, creating and resolving dissonances. Players can bend pitch, too, and employ natural tuning to great effect, leaning into those wide intervals for expressiveness and emotion. It is often said that, in Western music, harmony is emotion, but that is no less true of non-Western music. The difference is that in Western music, harmony has tended to be both functional and structural. Far from being tied to a tonic for the duration, a piece of music might begin there, before moving to other chords and keys, sometimes quite remote, finally returning to the home key (or sometimes not). But it can only do this because of the ironing out of natural tuning: equal temperament made all whole tones the same and, likewise, all semitones. This standardisation involved a considerable loss of melodic character and distinction with a concomitant loss of expressive ability, but the gain was significant.

Back to the keyboard one last time. Where naturally tuned scales were all different from one another, the equally tempered diatonic scale came in just two basic varieties, major and minor. That diatonic scale from C to C using only the white notes is called C major, its structure consisting of the intervals of two whole tones (C to D, D to E) followed by a semitone (E to F), then three whole tones (F to G, G to A, A to B) followed by another semitone (B to C). That is not only the structure of C major, but of the other eleven possible major scales. If you start on C sharp and employ the same distribution of whole tones and semitones, you will produce a scale of C sharp major – you're using black notes now as well as white, but it's the intervals between the notes that matter. It will be the same when you begin on any other of the twelve possible pitches. With natural tuning, these twelve major scales would have had different characteristics, in the context of which accidentals (notes foreign to a scale) would have sounded out of tune. This is why Tallis's *Spem in alium* stays in C major until just before the end, and why the sudden jump into A for the coda would have struck the singers and listeners as significant.

It was in the early seventeenth century, not long after Tallis's death, that European musicians began to experiment with equal temperament and the possibility of roaming freely from key to key within a single piece of music; but they met with resistance. The change was really brought about by the growing popularity of keyboard instruments. Singers and string players were used to adapting their tuning during a piece so as to avoid unwanted dissonance; in more chromatic music, they could sing or play a bit sharper here, a bit flatter there, to accommodate the flexibility of pitch. But you can't retune a harpsichord in the middle of a phrase, and with equal temperament you didn't have to.

In 1722, as though to demonstrate what was now possible, J.S. Bach composed the first of two books of keyboard music called *Das wohltemperierte Klavier* (The Well-Tempered Clavier), containing twenty-four preludes and fugues in each of the major and minor keys. Another book would follow in 1742. There is some debate about whether Bach employed or intended the strict equal temperament that became the norm after his death, but for keyboard instruments there was no going back, and neither was there for Western art music, which became wedded to the possibilities of structures built from shifting keys.

Mention of Bach leads to the other principal advantage of staff notation: counterpoint, which is a form of polyphony. The term 'polyphony' means many voices and all polyphonic music involves voices or instruments layered on top of each other and often moving at different speeds. Javanese and Balinese gamelan music is a good example of this, the lines in the percussion-dominated orchestra ranging from the punctuating tolls of the large gong to the fast, showy figuration of the xylophones. But such layering – dazzling and complex though it may be – is not quite counterpoint, the individual lines tending to stick to repeating rhythmic patterns. Furthermore, although gamelan developed its own notation as late as the nineteenth century, this was largely for archival purposes. It remains an orally transmitted music.

Another form of polyphony that isn't quite counterpoint might be New Orleans jazz. In the joyously hectic opening of 'Potato Head Blues' recorded in 1927 by Louis Armstrong and His Hot Seven, Johnny Dodds's clarinet swoops and swirls around the other layers of the music in a spontaneous display of counter-melodic invention, simultaneously poised and brilliant and seemingly effortless. But you could argue that this is embellishment more than counterpoint: take the clarinet away and the music, while less thrilling, would still work. Also, the Hot Seven are playing over chords that repeat as a cycle (known in jazz as 'changes'), so the music has a limited harmonic palette.

Truly contrapuntal music involves lines that work together harmonically while being both complementary and independent of each other in terms of melodic shape and rhythm. It began properly in the sixteenth century and reached a kind of apogee in the masses and motets of Giovanni Pierluigi da Palestrina (c. 1525–1594). Tallis's *Spem in alium*, although harmonically static, is a resplendent example of counterpoint. But Bach's keyboard music, particularly his fugues, brought new levels of complexity and virtuosity.

A fugue is a bit like a canon or a round (such as 'Frère Jacques' or 'Row, Row, Row Your Boat') in which several voices sing the same melodic line several beats apart from each other, their staggered entries creating a layered, polyphonic texture and generating harmony. The voices in a fugue, however, while their entries are staggered and their opening phrases similar,

The opening of Bach's six-part ricercar from *The Musical Offering*

usually start on different pitches and develop in individual ways that may involve moments of imitation but also new melodic invention. Not many people could improvise even a simple fugue, but Bach could, and a famous anecdote demonstrates the composer's skill in this, the limits of improvisation and the eventual necessity of writing things down.

In 1747, King Frederick the Great of Prussia, who was showing off his new fortepiano to Bach at the Potsdam Palace, presented the composer with a long and rather convoluted theme, possibly of his own devising, challenging his guest to improvise a three-part fugue on it. There can't have been many musicians capable of making up a three-part fugue on the spot, but Bach pulled it off. Disappointed, perhaps, Frederick now upped the ante, proposing a six-part fugue, at which point Bach demurred, explaining that he would have to take it away and work it out on paper. A couple of months later, he delivered *The Musical Offering*, an entire collection of pieces based on the king's theme, comprising some of the most complex contrapuntal music ever created, among them that six-part fugue or *Ricercar*, to give it the old-fashioned name Bach used.

Western musical notation allowed composers minute control over harmony and rhythm. This led to ever more ambitious harmonic structures in the symphonies of Beethoven, Bruckner and Mahler, the operas of Berlioz, Wagner and Verdi, the piano music of Robert Schumann and Liszt; and rhythmic complexity in Beethoven, Schumann, Stravinsky and later twentieth-century composers. The first movement of Ruth Crawford Seeger's String Quartet (1931) pits the four instruments against each other in rhythmic and thematic independence, while Conlon Nancarrow's piano music became so rhythmically intricate it required machines to play it. Notation allowed Mozart to pile five themes on top of each other at the end of his so-called 'Jupiter' symphony (No 41 in C), Charles Ives to arrange the exhilarating collision of hymn tunes and marching bands in his fourth symphony, and Iannis Xenakis to map his monolithic orchestral scores as an architect might create a blueprint (Xenakis had trained as an architect).

In general, Western art music has been less attentive to matters of timbre than many other forms of music. Notation for the Japanese shakuhachi, for example, often has more to say about the timbre and articulation of a note than about its pitch. But the richness of sonority created by a symphony orchestra – fifty to a hundred performers playing fifteen to twenty-five different sorts of instruments (not including the endless possibilities of percussion) – is unparalleled. In gagaku, there can be a range of instruments, but they aim to preserve their individual identities. Composers for symphony orchestras devoted themselves to the alchemy of orchestration, combining instrumental timbres in almost endless permutations, mixing and blending their colours to produce new shades.

The control of orchestration is another function of notation, so it is surprising that this was something of an add-on to the score. As late as the seventeenth century, composers did not allocate notes to particular instruments, or if they did their wishes were not recorded. We know the kinds of instruments that must have played in the orchestra accompanying Claudio Monteverdi's opera *L'Orfeo* (1607) from written descriptions and paintings; the score itself offers few clues.

When Bach presented six concertos to Christian Ludwig, Margrave of Brandenburg (younger brother of Frederick the Great) in 1721, their novelty was the ever-changing instrumentation of the pieces, with a different line-up of soloists for each work. No one before had employed and specified such lavish instrumentation. Bach was evidently hoping to impress the Margrave, perhaps with a view to finding employment, for he had copied up the concertos in his own hand, but there is no evidence the gift was acknowledged. Almost certainly, Christian Ludwig never heard the concertos (it's possible he couldn't afford the forces to perform them), the manuscripts remaining on a library shelf until they were discovered, published and performed in the middle of the nineteenth century.

It seems remarkable, given the subsequent popularity of the *Brandenburg* concertos, that they almost disappeared, but their survival is one more function of notation. While plenty of manuscripts have been lost or destroyed throughout history, the access we have to the musical creations of composers from hundreds of years ago is because so many have been preserved. Even if the music falls from favour or the performing materials are misplaced for a time, they can be rediscovered. Vivaldi's now-ubiquitous *Four Seasons* (published in 1725) is another example of a work that almost disappeared. Having been performed in the composer's lifetime and still quite well known in the later eighteenth century, it faded from view until the end of the Second World War, when it was recorded for the first time and went on to become the most famous baroque work of them all. It has now received more than a thousand commercial recordings, and you can encounter the music in an elevator.

* * *

> I am attracted only to music which I consider to be better than it can be performed. Therefore I feel (rightly or wrongly) that unless a piece of music presents a problem to me, a never-ending problem, it doesn't interest me too much.
>
> —Artur Schnabel (1882–1951), Austrian pianist and composer

Artur Schnabel was arguably the twentieth century's supreme interpreter of Beethoven's piano music, but his implication here is that no performance could ever do full justice to the potential of the score. As composers in the nineteenth century expanded their notions of what music might achieve, the scale of their works sometimes matching that of their ambitions, scores became more precise. Detailed dynamic marks allowed composers to stipulate relative degrees of volume – this note *forte*, that note *pianissimo*, this phrase getting louder, that phrase quieter – but it was all relative, all subject to interpretation. How loud, after all, is *forte*? Louder than *mezzo forte*; not as loud as *fortissimo*; a lot louder than *piano*: a performer still had to decide what loud meant. Naturally, context came into play – the context offered not only by the surrounding music, but by the instrument on which it was played and the room in which the performance took place. These decisions were down to the performer, as they still are, and are aspects of Schnabel's 'never-ending problem'.

Lorenzo Costa, *A Concert*

Another part of the problem was tempo, of vital importance in music because music is made in time. We see time beating in art works from ancient Egypt via the European Renaissance to the baroque period and beyond. Some of it is silent beating: in Luca della Robbia's fifteenth-century marble relief of Florentine choristers, the young men keep time on the shoulders of the boys. Some time-keeping evidently made a sound: two figures tap a marble ledge either side of a lutenist as they all sing from a book in Lorenzo Costa's fifteenth-century painting *A Concert*. But how did they know what the tempo should be?

There were some conventions. In Luca and Costa's times, and right through to Bach's, rhythm might indicate tempo. Often baroque composers would stipulate a dance form – sarabande, minuet, jig – and musicians would therefore know the appropriate tempo. But Italian terms such as *adagio*, *andante*, *allegro* and *presto* that had no obvious affiliation with the dancefloor led to the same sorts of problems encountered with those dynamic indications. How slow was *andante*? How fast was *allegro*?

There had been attempts to construct a metronome as early as the ninth century, when the Andalusian-born Berber scientist and musician Abbas ibn Firnas, whose main goal seems to have been to fly, is said to have invented one. There are no details. In the late 1500s, Galileo Galilei, who also had more important things on his mind, took a step towards the metronome with his studies of pendulums. But it was only in 1815 that a German inventor, Johann Nepomuk Maelzel, came up with the familiar, ticking contraption we still think of when we hear the word 'metronome', even if, these days, we tend to use a phone app to find a tempo.

Hoping for commercial endorsement, Maelzel made a present of one of his metronomes to Ludwig van Beethoven, and the composer didn't disappoint him, setting about applying metronome markings to many of his existing scores. Two years later, he published the tempos for his first eight symphonies (the ninth was yet to be composed).

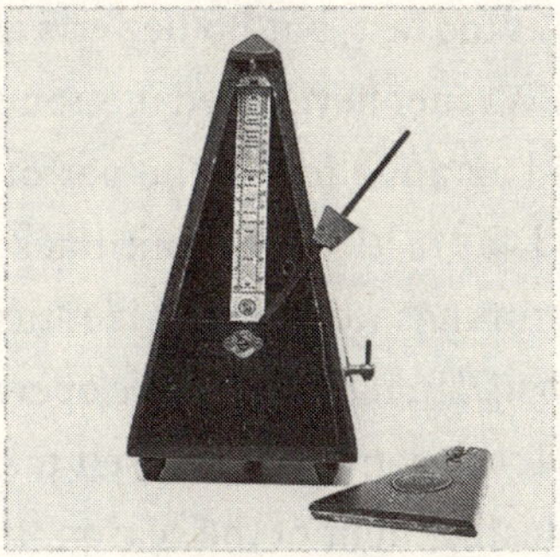

Maelzel metronome

Today, when we hear Beethoven's music played at the tempos he stipulated, it can surprise us. Particularly if we know some of the more famous recordings of the works in question, Beethoven's own speeds can seem too fast. It has been suggested that the composer's deafness, which was advanced by the time he acquired Maelzel's metronome, affected his judgement. A more plausible explanation, though, is that Beethoven never intended his music to be played at a single, unrelenting tempo, but for his metronome markings to indicate a starting speed that would be continually modified as the music ebbed and flowed. (We know this is exactly what Brahms wanted in performances of his music.)

But it's also true that performances of nineteenth-century music in general became slower during the twentieth century. Wagner's music presents an extreme example of this tendency. In 1966, when Pierre Boulez conducted Wagner's *Parsifal* at the Bayreuth Festival (an annual event established by Wagner in 1876 and devoted to his music), his tempos were widely criticised as too fast, but Boulez was able to prove otherwise. Although Wagner never used metronome markings in his scores, he did arrange for all the performances at Bayreuth to be timed, a practice that continues today. It turned out that Boulez's timings were almost identical to those of the first season of *Parsifal* in 1882, when the opera was conducted by Hermann Levi, the composer himself taking over for the final act on the closing night of the season. It was the performances in between that had slowed down; in 1951, Hans Knappertsbusch conducted the work with such plodding reverence that his performance lasted nearly an hour longer than either Levi's or Boulez's.

In the twentieth century, the writing of scores became, like much else in music, a matter of contention. On the one hand were composers whose work seemed to require ever more detailed notation; on the other, those who felt that such detail amounted to prescription. Gustav Mahler (1860–1911) was only a composer during his summer holidays; the rest of the time he was a star conductor – one of the first to have a transatlantic career – and his practical experience in concert halls and opera houses led him to annotate his music with unprecedented intricacy. He knew the orchestra intimately and, while he avoided metronome markings, fearing they would encourage performers to play mechanically, the scores of his symphonies are littered with verbal instructions in Italian and German regarding tempo and dynamics, articulation, timbre and expression.

But however remarkable the details in Mahler's scores must have seemed to his contemporaries, they are small beer compared to the scores of certain composers in the 1960s and beyond, when the English composer Brian Ferneyhough could give a player numerous pieces of information for just a single note, indicating not only pitch, duration and dynamic, but articulation, timbre, the position and direction of a bow on a string, followed by a different set of parameters for the next note. In contrast to this were the simple verbal instructions that set in motion the drone pieces of Pauline Oliveros and La Monte Young or the 'intuitive' music to which Karlheinz Stockhausen was briefly drawn in the early 1970s. Between these two extremes were artfully written scores by the likes of George Crumb, in which the staves themselves curved and curled expressively, no longer content simply to bear the dots of musical notation. And there were graphic scores – for example, those of Tom Phillips – employing diagrams and pictures. The composers of all these pieces would doubtless have argued that such scores were the clearest representations of their music and the simplest possible means of communicating their wishes to performers, and for all their differences of aesthetic and approach, they shared one thing. You couldn't sightread this music; you couldn't prop it up on a music stand and start singing or playing. These were scores that required time to digest.

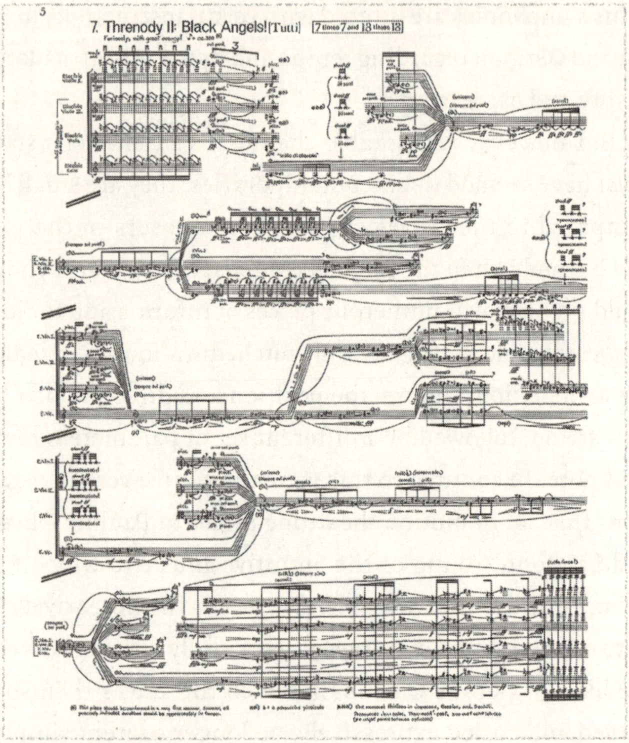

Threnody from George Crumb's *Black Angels*

Perhaps this is the place to point out that unlike most of the other sorts of music discussed in this book, Western art music – 'classical music' – is not a style. It is an endlessly adaptable system of notating sound such that a complex (or simple) piece can have repeat performances by one or four or a thousand performers and the music be entirely recognisable as Beethoven's 'Moonlight' sonata or Bartók's third string quartet or Mahler's eighth symphony, yet, because of Schnabel's 'never-ending' problems, it won't be exactly the same as any other performance of the piece. Moreover, while 'classical music' might contain elements of tradition and its practice has left us a vast catalogue of musical works, it demands to be added to. In order to be a tradition and not a museum, the catalogue must grow.

One aspect of the universal application of notation was the spread of the symphony orchestra beyond Europe and North America. Composers from Korea to Brazil, from Morocco to Japan brought their own voices to the orchestra and sometimes introduced instruments from outside the standard orchestral line-up. For example, in his orchestral piece *Réak* (1966), the Korean composer Isang Yun had massed winds and strings playing clusters of pitches to create an approximation of the saenghwang, the Korean mouth organ, while an assortment of drums and gongs added to the impression of a traditional aak orchestra (among other meanings, 'réak' is the Korean word for ritual). A year later, the Japanese composer Tōru Takemitsu, commissioned by the New York Philharmonic to write a piece celebrating its 125th birthday, added biwa and shakuhachi soloists to the orchestra for his startlingly dramatic piece *November Steps* (1967). But the symphony orchestra comes with its own culture, so it is always a two-way street: the Japanese composer's greatest influence was a Frenchman, Claude Debussy (1862–1918), who in turn had been influenced by what he knew of East and Southeast Asian music. It was in Debussy's music that Takemitsu immersed himself prior to composing *November Steps*; and before he began any major piece, it was his habit to listen to Bach's *St Matthew Passion*. There is no doubt that symphonic music is dominated, still, by the music of its European history.

Today, however, there are symphony orchestras all round the world. The Symphony Orchestra of India is based in Mumbai; the State Symphony Orchestra of the Democratic People's Republic of Korea in Pyongyang; the Vietnam Symphony Orchestra in Hanoi; the Syrian National Symphony Orchestra in Damascus; the Kimbanguist Symphony Orchestra in Kinshasa; and the National Symphony Orchestra of Peru in Lima. Egypt has its Cairo Symphony Orchestra; the Kampala Symphony Orchestra is in the Ugandan capital; and in Venezuela the Simón Bolivar Symphony Orchestra consists of players who grew up in some of the poorest neighbourhoods in Caracas. All these orchestras play the music of their local composers but also Beethoven and Debussy and the whole historical pantheon of Western music, and they are able to do so because of the work of an eleventh-century Benedictine monk, Guido.

But is it possible that all this orchestral music might be a manifestation of imperialism? It is a question that has exercised certain Western academics in the early twenty-first century. Have the people of India, North Korea, Vietnam, Syria, the Congo, Peru, Uganda, Egypt and Venezuela been duped into accepting some colonial attitude to music? We should probably ask them rather than the academics. Certainly this was the view that Mao Zedong expressed in 1966 at the start of China's Cultural Revolution when, for some reason, the music of Debussy was singled out as 'the dirt left behind' by Western imperialism. At the Shanghai Conservatory, its director, the composer He Luting, was tortured for his defence of the French composer's music and humiliated on national television. He stood his ground and survived, but some musicians did not. Lu Hongen, the conductor of the Shanghai Symphony Orchestra and a particular exponent of Beethoven, was among those executed (the following day his wife was invoiced for the bullet), while others took their own lives. By the time Mao died in 1976, ending the ten-year terror, all 500 pianos in the Shanghai Conservatory had been destroyed, and three years later, when the Chinese government invited the American violinist Isaac Stern to play concerts there, it proved impossible to find a working piano in the whole of Shanghai. Forty years on, everything had changed. Shanghai Conservatory was home to the He Luting Concert Hall, and in 2022, the China Musical Instrument Association estimated that the country was responsible for the manufacture of nearly 70 per cent of the world's pianos and more than 50 per cent of other Western instruments.

* * *

> To all printers, booksellers and other officers,
> ministers, and subjects, greetings. Know you,
> that we for the special affection and goodwill that
> we have and bear to the science of music and for
> the advancement thereof, by our letters patent

> dated the 12th of January, in the 17th year of our reign have granted full privilege and licence to our well beloved servants Thomas Tallis and William Byrd, two of the gentlemen of our chapel, and to the survivor of them, and to the assignees of them and over the survivor of them for eleven years next ensuing, to imprint any and so many as they will of set song or songs in parts, either in English, Latin, French, Italian, or other languages that may serve for music either in church or chamber, or otherwise to be either played or sung, and that they may rule and cause to be ruled by impression any paper to serve for printing or picking of any song or songs, and may sell and utter any printed books or papers of any song or songs, or any books or quires of such ruled paper imprinted.
>
> —Elizabeth by the grace of God, Queen of England, France and Ireland

Staff notation was not just for composers and orchestral players. Commercial music publishing had begun in the sixteenth century when, in 1575, Elizabeth I granted Tallis and his pupil William Byrd a licence – a monopoly, indeed – to publish their own and others' music, so ushering in new habits in domestic music-making, at least among the gentry. The singing of part songs and, in time, the playing of chamber music – viol consorts and, later, string quartets – became common pastimes throughout Europe. What made such music especially collegiate was that sets of vocal or instrumental parts seldom came with a full score. You bought the new string quartet parts by Haydn or Mozart, took them home to share with family or friends, and until you began to play had very little idea of the music as a whole. Fitting the parts together to reveal the music was like a parlour game.

Alongside such communal music-making, a more solitary sort was keyboard music. Harpsichords and clavichords gave way to drawing-room pianos, and these instruments grew in popularity and number. The piano became a standard piece of furniture in middle-class homes, where a mother or daughter could usually play the instrument with a degree of accomplishment. By the early twentieth century, upright pianos could also be found across Europe, the United States and farther afield in the homes of many working-class people. In colonial Australia, right from the start, the instrument was, to quote the title of Michael Atherton's book on the subject, 'a coveted possession'.

As piano ownership proliferated, so did musical literacy, helped by the rise of choral societies in the large cities that had grown up with the Industrial Revolution. They began in Germany, early in the nineteenth century, but quickly became a pan-European phenomenon. Sometimes numbering hundreds of members, these associations were cross sections of society, meeting each week to rehearse for their performances of Handel's *Messiah* or Felix Mendelssohn's *St Paul*. In England, where civic choirs had been a feature of national life since the eighteenth century, singers still used scores that showed only their own parts, the notation often employing the names of notes rather than dots on a stave. Choral societies also became caught up in nationalist movements, and this was reflected in their repertoires: immigrant communities from Europe took music with them to Canada, Australia and the United States.

A parallel phenomenon to the choral society was the brass band. Community bands with various combinations of instruments increased exponentially during the nineteenth century, but brass bands (sometimes called silver bands) were a strong tradition in industrial Britain, particularly in the north of England. Collieries, factories and mills purchased cornets, horns, euphoniums and tubas, in part to keep their workers out of pubs. There was nothing amateur-sounding about the best of these bands. Playing a repertoire that mixed original music with arrangements of classical pieces, operatic excerpts and popular tunes, bands competed to a high standard in regional and national contests, displaying a fervour for winning akin to that of their local football teams.

The brass-band world continues to have a remarkably strong culture that sets it apart from other amateur music-making. Huddersfield in West Yorkshire is its epicentre. Within a ten-mile radius, there are more than fifty bands of various levels, including the Black Dyke, Hammonds Saltaire and Brighouse & Rastrick bands. The town is also home to one of Britain's most famous amateur choirs, the Huddersfield Choral Society, founded in 1836. When, in 1978, the violinist Yehudi Menuhin played a solo recital in the Victorian splendour of Huddersfield Town Hall, he told his personal assistant, Philip Bailey, to sit in the audience and look around. What Bailey observed, as the violinist knew he would, was dozens of audience members following Menuhin's Bach and Bartók with scores.

'You can't get away with second best in this part of the world,' Menuhin told his assistant, attributing the audience's intense scrutiny to the region's bands and choral societies.

By the twentieth century, staff notation had become an international norm. It didn't replace tablature ('tabs'), but often coexisted on the same page, and this was especially important in the dissemination of sheet music of popular songs, which came with both simple piano accompaniments and 'tabs' for guitar or ukulele. This sort of sheet music was a quick way to learn a song for singing at home round the piano or in a pub, where in pre-jukebox days singalongs were a common form of entertainment.

It was also how hit songs were made, and the songs of the American composer Stephen Foster (1826–1864) are a good example. In the mid-nineteenth century, Foster's output included songs written for minstrel shows including 'Oh! Susanna' (complete with its reference to coming 'from Alabama with a banjo on my knee') and 'Camptown Races', before he came to specialise in parlour songs such as 'Jeanie with the Light Brown Hair', 'Hard Times Come Again No More' and 'Beautiful Dreamer'. While they never made their composer rich, Foster's songs became widely known in the United States and abroad and remain so today, well crafted, catchy, sentimental to a fault and with a strong whiff of the antebellum South. (In fact Foster, who was a northerner, went south only once in his lifetime – a steamboat trip to New Orleans for his honeymoon.)

Cover of 'Maple Leaf Rag'

Scott Joplin's rags, similarly, gained their popularity through sheet music. Joplin (c. 1868–1917) didn't begin the craze for ragtime, but his 'Maple Leaf Rag' (1899) was one of the best-known examples of the style and its sales guaranteed him an income for life and the time to work on his opera *Treemonisha*, completed in 1910 and published the following year at Joplin's expense. Reviewing *Treemonisha* – the score, that is, for there was no staging of it in the composer's lifetime – *The American Musician and Art Journal* praised the opera at length, insisting that it ushered in 'an entirely new phase of musical art'. It is worth adding that the publication of rags by Joplin and others allowed the music to travel to Europe, where it influenced the likes of Debussy, Erik

Satie and, later, Stravinsky, all of whom embraced the style on the basis of sheet music rather than recordings.

Even after the arrival of sound recording, printed scores maintained a hold on popular music. Songs were published and often simultaneously recorded by a number of artists. For example, Mabel Wayne's 'Little Man, You've Had a Busy Day', published in 1934 with words by Al Hoffman and Maurice Sigler, was recorded five times that same year by Elsie Carlisle, Paul Robeson, Isham Jones, Al Bowlly (with the Ray Noble Orchestra) and Emil Coleman. That the song became a hit was not down to a single performer so much as to its general familiarity and the availability of sheet music, which enabled the song to be sung round the family piano or by anyone with a ukulele.

After the Second World War, the publishing of sheet music continued alongside the growing record industry, but it was done differently. Hit songs were transcribed *ex post facto* and often inexpertly from recordings, leading to disappointed fans who found that their home performances of songs by the Beatles failed even to approximate the sound of the 'original', tied as that was to the sound of the Beatles' voices and guitars.

This is quite a moment in musical history, though it is seldom remarked upon. Where for Artur Schnabel there had been no performance of a Beethoven sonata as great as the sonata itself – no interpretation that could do full justice to the printed score – now there was no performance of a Beatles song that could match the Beatles' own. The original version of the 'Moonlight' sonata was on the page; the original version of 'Love Me Do' was the recording. The musical text had jumped ship.

Yet still sheet music continued to appear for pop, jazz and rock, and some of the publications were decidedly quixotic in their aim. Back in 1725, it is unlikely that the final version of the three-part fugue that appears in *The Musical Offering* matched the fugue Bach had made up on the spot for Frederick the Great. Apart from the composer's wish for second thoughts, it would have been impossible for Bach to recall every detail of his improvisation. It would be equally hard to recall, say, the details of a solo by John Coltrane or Frank Zappa if we didn't have sound recordings. But in addition to listening to *A Love Supreme* or *Hot Rats*, there was a desire on the part of some fans of jazz and rock to see the music written down – if not to play it themselves, then at least to learn how Coltrane and Zappa played it. But these transcriptions revealed nothing of the sort. Coltrane and Zappa, though both of them were highly musically educated, did not come from literary traditions. Their music, for the most part, was improvised, their ecstatic solos spontaneous inventions that were never the same twice: to see them written down, the intricacies rendered in hundreds of dots and complex rhythms, is to learn very little.

In *The Frank Zappa Guitar Book*, Zappa's bandmate Steve Vai transcribed a single measure of 'While You Were Out' as a guitar phrase of thirteen semiquavers (sixteenth notes) in the time of fourteen, over a drum pattern of three crotchet triplets in the time of two, followed by a septuplet. As a transcription of what we hear, it seems fairly accurate, but it was surely not in Zappa's thoughts as he improvised the solo, and one doubts he could have played it accurately from the notation. Although Zappa approved it and paid Vai a salary for his work, the transcription is next to pointless. When it came to composing music for orchestra and other large ensembles, something Zappa did increasingly in his later years, Guido of Arezzo's lines and dots were essential, but *The Frank Zappa Guitar Book* was a form of vanity publishing that made his music look more complex than it was.

The move from sheet music to sound recording in popular music – from written text to sonic text – changed the way music was made, the way it was appreciated and the way it was bought and sold. But then the very fact of music's being offered for sale had changed its nature over thousands of years.

3

MUSIC FOR SALE: PAYING THE PIPER FROM 1000 BCE TO THE PRESENT

ONE DAY IN 1934, FULTON ALLEN, known to history as Blind Boy Fuller, was playing his guitar on a street corner in the town of his birth: Wadesboro, North Carolina. He was an exponent of what has since come to be known as Piedmont blues, from the eastern foothills of the Appalachian Mountains, jauntier than the blues of Texas or the Mississippi, with a heavy thumb on the guitar's bottom string alternating with forefinger picking of the tune on the upper strings. There was an obvious connection to the agile left hand of stride piano, and the repertoire overlapped too, Piedmont blues being full of ragtime rhythms.

In the early twentieth century, blind African American blues musicians – singers, guitarists, harmonica players – could be heard on the streets of cities throughout much of the southern United States. Some had been blind since birth; others, like Fuller (who had started out as a labourer), had lost their sight as young men, putting an end to their earning a living unless they could play music. Most of them worked with sighted runners who looked after the collecting tin and, in some cases, played washboard. Among the best known were Blind Lemon Jefferson, Blind Blake, Reverend Gary Davies, Blind Willie Johnson and Blind Willie McTell, all born within five years of each other in the 1890s. Jefferson and Johnson were Texans, but the others, like Blind Boy Fuller, played in the Piedmont style.

Blind Boy Fuller

This particular day, as Fuller picked his way through dance tunes such as 'Step It Up and Go', he heard from across the way a spritely harmonica he failed to recognise. It belonged to Saunders Terrell, better known as Sonny Terry, also blind.

Forty years later, Sonny Terry recalled that he had heard Fuller's guitar 'whining' and 'wailing' in the distance, and asked his runner to find out who it was and invite him over to play, but at that moment Fuller's runner arrived to issue a similar invitation to Terry. In one version of the story, it was the albino washboard player Bull City Red that Fuller sent across the street. Over the following six years, before Blind Boy Fuller's death at the age of thirty-six, this trio of Fuller, Terry and Red would make a number of recordings together, including an especially infectious account of 'Step It Up and Go'.

* * *

> I became a professional at three. I would go around in the church playing songs like 'This Little Light of Mine' with a cup in my hand and people would put coins in. Even then, I knew I wasn't playing for free.
>
> —Carla Bley (1936–2023), American jazz composer, pianist and band leader

There is a tendency today for some to believe that music should be free, viewing copyright law as an outrage. We search for music online, we stream songs at will, we feel we should be able to post our favourites on social media; after all, aren't we doing the musician a favour? The attitude is not new, even if the details might belong to our time. Most of us are involved in music at some level – at the very least as listeners – and most regard it as a hobby. It's a short step to believing that musicians, too, are hobbyists. Try telling that to the likes of Blind Boy Fuller.

Itinerant buskers are the most clear-cut instance of the professional musician. We listen to their performances and toss money into their tins. These musicians must stay on the move – if they remain in one place too long, their paying public will tire of the same old songs. This has been the way of things for hundreds of years and in most cultures of the world, and often the musicians have been sightless.

Their origins are obscure, but it is thought that from at least the Muromachi period (beginning in the mid-fourteenth century), blind women known as goze were active in Japan, playing the shamisen, singing traditional songs and telling stories for money as they travelled from village to village, even in the dead of winter. By the beginning of the seventeenth century, there was an official guild for the goze. Around the same time, during the Cossack Hetmanate in Ukraine, the kobza, another lute-like instrument, was played by blind kobzari to accompany the reciting of epic poetry, often recalling famous Cossack military victories. In Ireland, there was a tradition of travelling blind harpers, the most famous and successful of them Turlough O'Carolan (Toirdhealbhach Ó Cearbhalláin) (1670–1738). O'Carolan's reputation was such that his tunes, which might otherwise have been subsumed by his country's vast oral tradition, survived with his name attached and were transcribed and published after his death as quasi-classical pieces.

Blind itinerant musicians feature in a number of northern European ballads. In 'The Two Sisters' – multiple versions of which exist in Scandinavia, Scotland and England – a blind harper fashions an instrument from the washed-up remains of a young woman drowned by her sister, making the frame from her bones and stringing it with her hair. The harper proceeds to play at the wedding of the murderous sibling, the instrument itself suddenly gaining the power of speech with which it denounces the culprit.

Komusō

Something like metaphorical blindness was practised by a guild of mendicant monks in Japan. From the early seventeenth century until the mid-nineteenth, the komusō – literally monks or priests of nothingness or emptiness – belonging to the Fuke sect of Zen Buddhism played shakuhachi with reed baskets on their heads. The players were sighted, the purpose of the baskets – and of the blowing – to obliterate the monks' egos. In time, the baskets increased in size until the faces of the players were totally obscured, their consequent anonymity enabling a side hustle in the form of spying for the state. In the Edo period, travel in Japan was restricted, but the monks of nothingness were given special dispensation to wander the countryside playing and begging for alms (money or rice), in exchange for reporting suspicious activity.

In modern parlance, the word 'troubadour' has become almost a synonym for an itinerant musician, but for the most part the historical troubadours of medieval Provence shunned the peripatetic life. Along with their female equivalents, the trobairitz, their northern equivalents, the trouvères, and the German minnesingers, whom they influenced, these poet–composers – singer–songwriters before the fact – wrote of courtly love, and where better to do that than at a court? They might have moved from one ducal household to another, but what they were after was the longest stay possible and a stipend to match. In the early thirteenth century, the Provençal troubadours were mortally wounded by the Albigensian Crusade and then finished off, a century later, by the Black Death, but not before the tradition had produced hundreds of examples of lyric poetry in the old Occitan language and in many cases tunes to fit them.

Six hundred years later, in nineteenth-century Mexico, mariachi bands, which we also think of as itinerant, were similarly ensconced in Latin America's answer to the medieval castle, the hacienda. Having long since taken over the instruments of their Spanish colonial masters – violins, harps and guitars of varying size (trumpets came later) – mariachis functioned as in-house entertainment at their country estates. Like the troubadours, they might occasionally have moved from one hacienda to another, but steady employment was their aim. The Mexican Revolution put an end to the haciendas and their feudalism, and from around 1920 the mariachis were obliged to become itinerant, eventually converging on Mexico City. At the start, mariachi music had been mostly instrumental, but singing became more important during the post-revolutionary period, and often the lyrics were topical, a mixture of news and commentary, in the manner of the calypso singers of Trinidad and Tobago.

The singer-composer as storyteller and newscaster is a familiar trope in traditional music, although this only describes some of the functions of the griot or jali in Mali, Senegal and other parts of West Africa. The hereditary profession also involves the preservation of histories – including family histories – and so griots, though often itinerant, also have close ties to their communities (whose stories and traditions they guard) and in the past were important figures at court, their duties including the performance of that pan-African musico-literary form, the praise song, exalting their kings and their gods. Indeed, their training both as singers and as instrumentalists involved divine intervention in the form of a tutor–spirit. Royal patronage of griots in Africa is largely a thing of the past and today they are more likely to be singers at weddings and funerals or, in some cases, internationally famous on the festival circuit, which is what happened to Malian singer Salif Keita, and to Youssou N'Dour and Baaba Maal of Senegal. Still the roots run deep.

'Everyone uses the music everyday,' Baaba Maal said in 1999, 'everywhere in society the music is like a reference. The musicians, the historians, the story tellers: they are still very, very important, because a lot of people haven't been to school and they can't read newspapers.'

* * *

> And he set the Levites in the house of the Lord
> with cymbals, with psalteries, and with harps,
> according to the commandment of David, and of
> Gad the king's seer, and Nathan the prophet: for
> so was the commandment of the Lord by
> his prophets.
>
> And the Levites stood with the instruments of
> David, and the priests with the trumpets.
>
> And Hezekiah commanded to offer the burnt
> offering upon the altar. And when the burnt
> offering began, the song of the Lord began also
> with the trumpets, and with the instruments
> ordained by David King of Israel.
>
> —2 Chronicles 29: 25–27

Before David was king of Israel, he was a professional musician, a harpist and composer, credited with writing a number of psalms. That's according to the Book of Samuel in the Hebrew Bible, though there is scant corroborating evidence. But for centuries, royal and religious patronage (sometimes indistinguishable) were common sources of employment, and David, musician to King Saul, is at the very least a symbol of the sort of relationship that existed from ancient times to early modern, in Asia, Africa and Europe, from the Chinese musicians in yǎyuè orchestras to griots to the twelfth-century composers who worked under the patronage of Notre-Dame de Paris.

It might seem to us that a church or court composer, while keeping warm and dry and eating well, is unlikely to have been at music's cutting edge. But the Notre-Dame composers demonstrate otherwise, as does the career of Jean-Baptiste Lully (1632–1687) at the Palace of Versailles during the reign of Louis XIV. An ambitious (some would say ruthless) figure in baroque music, Lully became a violinist at the royal palace around the age of twenty. Six years older than the king (who had acceded to the throne aged four), Lully progressed quickly, first composing music for dancing and then for Versailles's opera theatre, in collaboration with the playwright Molière. In the process, he forged the beginnings of a French style (Lully himself had been born in Italy) complete with swaggering overtures, characterised by double-dotted rhythms that to modern ears have an undeniably regal sound. His operas are full of dance metres and lively tempos (the king liked to dance), and his word setting was peculiarly responsive to the sound and rhythm of the French language. These developments were perhaps more cosmetic than structural, but Lully's story shows that having a day job did not necessarily stunt a composer's originality.

The case of Joseph Haydn, meanwhile, demonstrates that with an enlightened boss, a composer's imagination might run free.

* * *

> My prince was always pleased with my works. Not only did he encourage me with constant approval, but as conductor of an orchestra I was able to experiment, to notice what produced a good effect and what weakened it. I could therefore improve, change, add or subtract, and be as bold as I pleased. There was no one [at Esterháza] to confuse or annoy me, so I was obliged to be original.
>
> —Joseph Haydn (1732–1809), Austrian composer

In 1761, the 29-year-old Haydn arrived at Schloss Esterházy in Eisenstadt, south of Vienna, to take up work for the Esterházy family. As Kapellmeister, or director of music, he wore a servant's livery and occupied a position in the household on a par with that of the cook. His job was partly managerial and partly artistic, and included conducting the orchestra and singers, playing chamber music (sometimes with his employer) and composing a vast number of new works.

Prince Nikolaus Esterházy was a music lover and a player of the baryton, an instrument like a bass viol but with sympathetic strings, and one of the drawbacks of Haydn's employment was his obligation to provide music for this instrument. Haydn composed for Nikolaus no fewer than 126 trios for viola, cello and baryton, before the prince put away childish things and abruptly became a devotee of opera, at which point Haydn turned his hand to writing for the stage. Five years after Haydn's arrival in Eisenstadt, Nikolaus had rebuilt the family's palace, Esterháza, on swampland in Fertőd – even further from Vienna. The new palace included two opera theatres and was Haydn's home until Nikolaus's death in 1790.

Esterháza

Today the world has forgotten about Haydn's operas and, in the absence of instruments on which to play them, the 126 baryton trios gather dust; but Esterháza was the making of the composer. You might think that, writing all that baryton music, Haydn wouldn't have had time for much else, but he composed more than sixty symphonies for Nikolaus, as well as string quartets, piano sonatas and piano trios. While the music was produced to order, Haydn was free to write in any way he chose. In Nikolaus, Haydn had a fan who was content to see what his Kapellmeister came up with each week, and new ideas were welcomed.

Histories of Western music always used to call Haydn the 'father of the symphony' and 'father of the string quartet'. He wasn't. Not quite. These musical genres – the symphony, the quartet, the sonata – were already coming into existence in the middle of the eighteenth century. But while Haydn didn't invent the forms, he can fairly be said to have modernised them, completing, in his lifetime, 106 symphonies and sixty-eight string quartets. Before Haydn, a symphony could be almost any piece of orchestral music; after him, it was a four-movement work lasting roughly half an hour. Not bad for an 'imperial lackey', as Wagner would later refer to him.

Despite his isolation at Esterháza, Haydn's music travelled and his reputation grew. Nikolaus allowed him to send works to publishers, and his new piano sonatas and string quartets were widely played in people's homes; his symphonies were heard not only in Vienna, but in Paris and London. He was permitted to take commissions, too, and in 1785 accepted an invitation from Joseph Bologne, Chevalier de Saint-Georges, to write a set of six symphonies for the private orchestra of which Saint-Georges was chief conductor, Le Concert de la Loge Olympique. In fact, Saint-Georges was acting as broker for the Comte d'Ogny, a French aristocrat, amateur cellist and

Freemason, who had founded his own Masonic lodge – the Olympic Lodge – specifically to put on concerts. This commission gave Haydn access to an orchestra twice the size of that at Esterháza. Saint-Georges, a Creole man born in the colony of Guadeloupe to a wealthy French planter and an enslaved Senegalese woman, was a violinist, conductor and composer who had modelled some of his own music on Haydn's and had already done much to popularise Haydn's work in Paris. These grand, new symphonies – the so-called Paris symphonies – helped build Haydn's reputation in the French capital. Even Marie Antoinette came to the premiere of the symphony in B flat, thereafter known as *La Reine* (The Queen).

In 1790, when Nikolaus's son, Prince Anton, succeeded his father, Haydn, pushing sixty, was suddenly able to capitalise on his fame. Anton disbanded the house orchestra, being interested neither in music nor in living at Esterháza. He continued to pay Haydn a small salary, and the composer was free to travel. A German violinist and impresario, Johann Peter Salomon, seized the chance and commissioned six symphonies for his London orchestra; Haydn went to London to conduct them. It was the first time he had seen the sea. On 12 March 1791, the day after the first concert, the *Morning Chronicle* opined that 'Haydn should be an object of homage and even idolatry; for like our own Shakespeare, he moves and governs the passions at his will'. Something close to idolatry ensued. In short order Salomon commissioned a further six symphonies and Haydn returned to London in 1794. From servant to superstar!

But Haydn was not finished with the Esterházys. During his second English sojourn, he learnt that Prince Anton had died and would be succeeded by his son, the 29-year-old Nikolaus II. A soldier and collector of fine art, Nikolaus was also a music lover, and Haydn returned to work once more as Kapellmeister, though now part-time. Although this Nikolaus was a thoroughgoing philanderer, his musical tastes were devotional. He requested an annual mass for his wife's name day (a form of penance, perhaps) and Haydn composed six of these. But Haydn's relationship with Nikolaus was not easy. He had returned to the Esterházys' employ the most famous composer in Europe with an honorary doctorate from Oxford; he wasn't about to be treated as a servant again.

In joining the household staff of an aristocratic family, Haydn, as a young man, had followed in his mother's footsteps. Prior to her marriage, Maria Koller had cooked for the Harrach family at their castle in Rohrau. Haydn's father was a wheelwright. This is important to understand. In the twenty-first century, European classical music has gained a reputation for being high-status, and certainly in the eighteenth century it was paid for and heard by the 'Nobility and Gentry' (to quote Salomon's advertisement for Haydn's first London concert). But the composers of this music came from trade. Bach, Mozart, Beethoven, Liszt, Brahms, Richard Strauss and Stravinsky all had fathers who were themselves jobbing musicians. Lully came from a family of millers, Handel's father was a barber, Smetana's a brewer, and Dvořák's a butcher who played a bit of zither on the side. Schubert's father was a coachman and later an innkeeper. Verdi's and Mahler's fathers were also innkeepers; Mahler's paternal grandmother had been a street pedlar. Robert Schumann's, Schoenberg's and Debussy's fathers were shopkeepers (selling books, shoes and china, respectively). Wagner's father, who died when the boy was six months old, was a clerk in the Leipzig police department; Wagner's stepfather an actor. Edward Elgar's father was a piano tuner. In a few cases, the trade was more like a calling – Chopin's father taught French, Bruckner's was a village schoolmaster, and

Brahms's birthplace in Hamburg, c. 1910. The building was destroyed by Allied bombing in World War II.

Bartók's was the principal of an agricultural college. Tchaikovsky's and Ravel's fathers were engineers. Berlioz's and Sibelius's fathers were physicians.

The point is that these composers were raised in households where skill, hard work and service were valued and money was sometimes tight; and, as boys, they were given educations generally denied their sisters. Just as their fathers would have served apprenticeships, so did the sons, composition passed on – as it mostly still is – by a working professional to a sort of intern. This alone might explain the dearth of female composers. But even those girls who secured a musical education were not guaranteed a career.

* * *

> I cannot help considering it a sign of talent that I do not give it up, though I can get nobody to take an interest in my efforts.
>
> —Fanny Mendelssohn Hensel (1805–1847),
> German composer

Of classical music's most famous composers, only Felix Mendelssohn (1809–1847) really came from money. His father, Abraham Mendelssohn, was a banker, and his grandfather was the philosopher Moses Mendelssohn. The fact that the family had brains in addition to wealth ensured that not only Felix but also his equally gifted older sister Fanny got a good education that included musical training.

The siblings' creativity was unstoppable; they wrote songs, piano pieces and chamber music as well as choral works and, in Felix's case, symphonies and concertos. Everyone recognised their talents but, hidebound by convention, the family refused to allow Fanny to publish her music. On her fourteenth birthday, her father wrote to her that while music might well become the eleven-year-old Felix's profession, she would have to settle for its being an 'ornament' in her life. Felix concurred, agreeing that Fanny might publish some of her songs under his name, an arrangement uncovered, in time, by none other than Queen Victoria. Felix was a favourite of the English monarch, who welcomed him, on one visit to London, with the good news that she had been learning his songs. When he asked if she would choose one to sing for him, she picked 'Italien', which was by Fanny. Felix couldn't brazen it out. 'I had to confess,' he wrote to his mother.

Fanny was being kept from a career by her gender and her class. The Mendelssohn family couldn't countenance her name being associated with a trade. It would not have been respectable. Yet hope eventually arrived in the form of Wilhelm Hensel, whom Fanny married in 1829. For many women, marriage would have marked the end of all aspirations to a career, but Hensel encouraged Fanny's work and its publication. The 1830s were taken up with the birth of her son and two subsequent stillbirths, coupled with a loss of confidence in her creativity, brought on, as much as anything, by Felix's lack of support. But Fanny rallied, and by the 1840s she was composing again. In 1846, she published – under her married name – a group of six songs designated 'Opus 1', along with a small volume of piano pieces, with the Berlin publishing house Bote & Bock. Fanny died the following year, aged forty-one, after which Felix saw to the publication of a handful of her other pieces. Within a year he, too, was dead.

Fanny Mendelssohn Hensel composed more than 450 pieces of music, mostly songs and piano solos. So why do we know so few of them and so little of the music of nineteenth-century women in general? Nineteenth-century literature would be unthinkable without Charlotte, Emily and Anne Brontë, Jane Austen, George Eliot and Elizabeth Gaskell (to name only novelists writing in English). Where were their composer equivalents?

As Fanny Mendelssohn knew, there was a double bind at work. For a girl to receive musical training in early-nineteenth-century Europe or the United States she had to be of a relatively high social rank, but then she couldn't ply her trade as a composer without risking disgrace. Female novelists and poets, by contrast, wrote at home and published either pseudonymously – in the case of Eliot and the Brontë sisters, adopting male identities – or anonymously, like Austen. What was to stop musically talented women doing the same? To be a successful composer of opera, oratorio or orchestral music, you might have required a public persona, but you could have written songs and piano pieces and parcelled them off to a publisher without ever showing your face. It must surely have been easier to publish a song or a piano piece than *Middlemarch*.

*

There was another problem. Something had happened to European music at the start of the nineteenth century that made it harder to be a professional composer without the rigorous training that was being denied to most women: in a word, Beethoven.

Between his two London trips, Haydn had given some lessons to the younger man, and in Beethoven's early sonatas, trios and string quartets we may recognise elements of his teacher's style. This did not last. By 1805 and the first performance of his third symphony, the *Eroica,* it was clear that Beethoven's music was of a different nature to Haydn's. Without wishing to suggest that Haydn's symphonies were interchangeable, there was certainly an assembly line approach to their production; he could hardly have written more than a hundred of them otherwise. In comparison, Beethoven composed just nine symphonies and only sixteen string quartets – less than a quarter of Haydn's total. The reason for this was that Beethoven's works were more ambitious. When we listen to one of Haydn's symphonies or quartets, we enter Haydn's world. But with Beethoven we enter the world of the piece and, notwithstanding the composer's fingerprints, it's a new world every time. Of course, this was to do with imagination, but it was also about technique. With any great composer, it is hard to separate the two, and Beethoven's approach to technique – the player's as well as his own – was as advanced as the music must have seemed to his contemporaries. Haydn's music could be performed by talented amateurs; much of Beethoven's could not.

* * *

> There is a lady in Vienna . . . who has been practising your B flat sonata for a month and she still can't play the beginning.
>
> —Carl Czerny (1791–1857), Austrian composer, to Ludwig van Beethoven

In Czerny's remark, written in one of the deaf composer's conversation books, we sense both astonishment and a certain amount of glee. Most Viennese ladies played the piano, and they expected to be able to play the latest sonatas tolerably well. But in Beethoven's Piano Sonata in B flat, Op. 106, known as the *Hammerklavier*, this lady had met more than her match. Even if she'd mastered the beginning, she'd have found yet more daunting challenges thrown up by the 45-minute work – at the time, the longest piano sonata ever composed. Had she made it to the last movement, its gargantuan fugue would surely have brought her undone. The level of virtuosity demanded by this piece would still defeat most amateur pianists. This was not drawing-room music, but a grand construction requiring a concert hall and a pianist with the most formidable technique: in short, a professional. Nearly two decades after the sonata's composition, Franz Liszt gave the first public performance we know of. This was the world Fanny Mendelssohn could not enter.

* * *

> Do not believe . . . that the artistic career is more accessible to my sex. This is a grave error. The steps are infinitely more difficult, and the good fellowship, which helps so many artists, is in a way shut out from a woman who has the good – or the ill – luck to be born a musician!
>
> —Augusta Holmès (1847–1903),
> Irish–French composer

The women from history whose music we hear today were often the daughters of musicians, receiving training from childhood and having little social status to lose. Francesca Caccini (1587–1640) was the daughter of the composer Giulio Caccini; Barbara Strozzi (1619–1677) the adopted (and probably biological) daughter of the Venetian poet and librettist Giulio Strozzi. Both women were singers as well as composers. The French composer and harpsichordist Élisabeth Jacquet de La Guerre (1665–1729) was born into a family of harpsichord makers; Harriet Wainwright (c. 1766–1843) came from generations of English church organists, although she herself was a singer as well as a composer. Louise Farrenc (1804–1875) was the daughter not of a musician, but of a sculptor; Clara Schumann (1819–1896) had pianists as parents, and her mother was also a singer. Pauline Viardot (1821–1910), whose father was a tenor, and who herself became one of the most celebrated opera singers of the nineteenth century, composed chamber music, songs and little drawing-room operas (three of them with librettos by the Russian novelist Turgenev), though never as a commercial enterprise. Cécile Chaminade (1857–1944), also from a musical family, was very much the professional composer, her music performed and published in her lifetime. She was even made a chevalier of the Legion of Honour, although, with the exception of a flute concertino, she was rapidly forgotten after her death. The same happened to Florence Price (1887–1953), born of African American heritage in Arkansas, where her mother was a music teacher. Her first symphony (of four) was played in 1933 by the Chicago Symphony Orchestra in a program called 'The Negro in Music'.

It was feminist scholars who unearthed these and other forgotten names and their music, and much of it has only recently been revived and recorded, a project that continues. These women tended to write in rather conservative styles, and perhaps this made them easier to dismiss in the progress-obsessed twentieth century. Lili Boulanger (1893–1918) and her older sister Nadia (1887–1979) were exceptions to the rule. Like the others, they had musical backgrounds – they were the daughters of a French composer and teacher and his former singing student, a Russian princess – but Lili in particular had a distinctive style that might have become even more distinctive had she lived as long as her sister. The death of this young woman at the age of twenty-four was inevitably overshadowed by Debussy's death just ten days later, yet hearing Lili's music today one recognises a voice with little or no obvious influence from her older compatriot. Indeed, in a work such as *D'un soir triste* (1918) we hear a pre-echo of the kind of music Henri Dutilleux (1916–2013) would go on to write in the later twentieth century – multi-hued, chromatic and mystical. Nadia Boulanger more or less gave up composition after Lili's death, devoting her long life to conducting, teaching and guarding her sister's legacy. Her pupils included composers as different from one another as Aaron Copland, Elliott Carter, Thea Musgrave, Philip Glass, Quincy Jones and Burt Bacharach.

* * *

> When I was young, comparatively few women worked.
>
> —Elisabeth Lutyens (1906–1983), English composer

Elisabeth Lutyens's remark requires context. She made it in 1962, speaking to the Canadian composer R. Murray Schafer for his book *British Composers in Interview*. Lutyens is the only woman in that volume – her given name misspelt – and Schafer asked her why she thought there had been so few female composers in history. Lutyens's reply betrays her aristocratic upbringing; when she says 'few women worked', she means that in the Edwardian England into which she was born, women seldom had professions. (The census of 1901 records that nearly a third of British women were in paid employment, more than

40 per cent of them working as domestic servants, with another 40 per cent in other service jobs or factories.)

Even so, Lutyens makes an important point, one that underlines the fact that composition was not only a vocation but a job; and as a professional composer in the mid-twentieth century, Lutyens knew all about hard work. She composed more than 160 official opuses, along with a vast amount of incidental music for theatre, radio, television and film; she was the first British woman to compose the score of a feature film, a more male-dominated medium even than the concert hall. But her successes were hard won. By 1941, she was raising four children under the age of ten from two marriages, while battling depression and alcoholism. What's more, as the first composer in Britain to adopt Schoenberg's twelve-tone technique (as early as the 1930s), her music hardly courted popularity. It did, however, seem to suit the string of horror movies she scored from the mid-1950s.

What Lutyens's answer to Schafer's question misses is the fact that in the early twentieth century, there were already successful female composers. Back in the seventeenth century, the Caccinis and Strozzis had been locally successful, and Strozzi is said to have published more music than anyone else in her lifetime, but success in the modern world was a different matter and Lutyens's compatriot Ethel Smyth (1858–1944) experienced some of that. In 1906, the year of Lutyens's birth, Smyth's opera *The Wreckers* received its first production in Berlin, followed by performances in Prague and then a season in London at Covent Garden, conducted by Thomas Beecham. An earlier one-act opera, *Der Wald* (The Forest), had also had its premiere in Berlin, prior to performances at Covent Garden and, in 1903, the Metropolitan Opera in New York, where it was the last opera by a woman for 113 years.

* * *

> This little woman writes music with a masculine hand and has a sound and logical brain, such as is supposed to be the especial gift of the rougher sex. There is not a weak or effeminate note in *Der Wald*, nor an unstable sentiment.
>
> —an anonymous review in *The Telegraph*, New York 1903

A critic's condescension aside (and there was more where that came from), Smyth was a significant national and international figure. Her fifteen-minute overture to *The Wreckers* was included in every season but one of the London Promenade concerts between 1913 and 1933, and the opera was revived in her lifetime and beyond. If her fame waned, which in the later twentieth century it certainly did, it might have been because her music didn't sound especially modern (in comparison to Lutyens's, for instance). The motivic writing of Wagner and the pictorialism of Strauss are never far away in Smyth's music, and after the Second World War, this was not what critics or promoters wanted in 'modern' composers.

Perhaps this also explains the similar neglect that befell the music of Samuel Coleridge-Taylor (1875–1912), a younger contemporary of Smyth who enjoyed considerable fame in both the United Kingdom and the United States. He was the son of an English woman and a West African Krio man, a physician who had found it impossible to gain a toehold in London's medical profession and returned to Sierra Leone, unaware he had fathered a child. Samuel's mother's family was musical and literary. It was she who added 'Coleridge' to plain Samuel Taylor, in honour of one of her favourite poets.

Coleridge-Taylor was exceptionally gifted and as a young composer came to the attention of Edward Elgar, who recommended him to his publisher ('far and away the cleverest fellow going amongst the younger men') and to the Three Choirs Festival, a bastion of provincial English music. Still in his early twenties, Coleridge-Taylor composed *Hiawatha's Wedding Feast*, a cantata based on Longfellow's epic poem *The Song of Hiawatha*. It was a triumph and quickly became a staple of English choral societies, rivalling Handel's *Messiah* in popularity (in England alone there were 200 performances of it in its first six years). A sequel was composed and then another, along with a new overture for the whole trilogy, for which the composer borrowed Longfellow's title. The first complete performance of *The Song of Hiawatha* was in Birmingham in 1901, where it eclipsed the previous year's poorly prepared premiere of Elgar's *The Dream of Gerontius*.

Coleridge-Taylor's success soon spread to the United States, the composer himself making three tours there to conduct his music, the first including a visit to the White House to meet Theodore Roosevelt. It was unusual for a US president to receive a guest of mixed race, and undoubtedly part of the composer's success in the States was the celebrity he enjoyed among African Americans.

Hiawatha at the Royal Albert Hall, c. 1930

For all that, Coleridge-Taylor died in poverty. Prior to the first performance, he had sold his rights to *Hiawatha's Wedding Feast* for a sum of fifteen guineas, and he received nothing more for the hundreds of thousands of scores sold. On learning the financial status of the composer's widow and children,

King George V awarded her an annual pension of a hundred pounds. In 1914, two years after Coleridge-Taylor's death and partly inspired by the circumstances of his family, the Performing Right Society was formed to collect royalties on performances of a composer's work.

Perhaps the greatest measure of Coleridge-Taylor's fame – and from this distance it is hard to credit – came more than a decade after his death, with the annual *Hiawatha* festivals staged by his son (himself named Hiawatha) in London's Royal Albert Hall. The hall seats nearly 6000 people and each festival ran for two weeks; the first took place in 1924 and they continued until the outbreak of the Second World War. *Hiawatha's Wedding Feast* was still enjoying performances in England as recently as the 1970s. But then its star faded.

The racism faced by musicians of colour was (and still is) as real as the obstacles placed in women's paths by a patriarchal society but, given the sustained popularity once enjoyed by *Hiawatha's Wedding Feast* and *The Wreckers*, racism and sexism alone cannot explain their dwindling reputations. Like Smyth's music, Coleridge-Taylor's smacked of the nineteenth century; in its tuneful ebullience, *Hiawatha's Wedding Feast* owed much to Smetana and Dvořák, no doubt endearing it to those choral societies but, after the war, coming to seem quaintly conservative to critics, broadcasters and promoters. At this point in its history, Western art music had run into a paradox in which genuinely popular music was being displaced by something that was less popular; but more of that in Chapter Four.

* * *

> It is good medicine to go to a concert hall and
> forget the harshness of what's going on.
> —Itzhak Perlman (b. 1945), Israeli violinist

The Hanover Square Rooms in which Haydn's London symphonies were first played would seem foreign to a modern concertgoer, and so would the eighteenth-century audience's concert etiquette. Salomon's 'Nobility and Gentry' had bought five-guinea subscriptions to his seasons, and they were there, as much as anything, to be seen. Audience members would chat throughout performances, bursting into spontaneous applause at a particularly arresting musical gesture, as audiences still do for jazz or Indian classical music. The Hanover Square Rooms were purpose-built for music and fashionable because of their novelty. In the 1790s the only other place like it in Europe was the Gewandhaus in Leipzig. Public concerts had taken place in Paris throughout much of the eighteenth century, but the so-called Concert Spirituel – a series of public concerts that had begun in 1725 – was housed in the Tuileries Palace. More commonly, music was still performed in rich people's homes, in dance halls and in theatres, where it crossed over with opera. In fact, the last three of Haydn's London symphonies were presented in the King's Theatre, really an opera house, for a larger and more varied audience. This was the theatre in which George Frideric Handel had presented twenty-five operas between 1711 and 1734, returning in 1738 and

1739 with four more, so it had a track record in the promotion of music to a paying audience.

In early eighteenth-century London, opera had been big, if precarious, business – Handel's opera company went bust twice. Still, the fame Handel enjoyed was unlike that of any composer before him. Among other distinctions, he was the first composer in history to have a biography written of him. Later in the century, opera would bring similar fame to Mozart in Vienna, then Verdi in nineteenth-century Milan, and Wagner in Dresden and Munich. In 1876, Wagner opened his own festival theatre in Bayreuth, designed to present his work under ideal circumstances. Opera audiences chatted as much as concertgoers until it occurred to Wagner to dim his theatre's house lights, thereby directing the spectator's gaze to the stage. The practice quickly caught on in theatres around the world.

From the start, opera singers had a cachet similar to today's film stars and sporting heroes. They were mobbed in the street and gained fame beyond their singing. Before the Three Tenors, there was Jenny Lind, the Swedish Nightingale, who sang *bel canto* roles in operas by Bellini and Donizetti and made her debut at the Leipzig Gewandhaus in a concert conducted by Felix Mendelssohn. This was followed by a triumphant tour of the United States, where she was managed by P.T. Barnum of the Barnum & Bailey Circus.

Individual operas, too, became enormously popular, and the craze for Wagner was especially wholehearted in fin-de-siècle Paris. Special trains ran to Bayreuth during the annual festival of Wagner's music and reputedly there were themed brothels where you could order characters from the *Der Ring des Nibelungen* (The Ring of the Nibelung) – a Rhinemaiden, say, or a Valkyrie. Wagner's contemporary, Verdi, found himself a figurehead for the Risorgimento, both before and after Italy's unification in 1861. His operas might have been set in Babylon (*Nabucco*), Scotland (*Macbeth*), Spain (*Il trovatore*) or Egypt (*Aida*), but Verdi's audiences knew that those famous choruses for Hebrew slaves or Spanish gypsies were *really* about them. It helped that the composer's name was an acronym for Vittorio Emanuele Re d'Italia (Victor Emanuel, King of Italy). When Italians shouted 'Viva Verdi!' it wasn't always possible to tell if they were opera lovers or nationalists. Usually they were both. And the composer's success wasn't restricted to Italy. Like Wagner's operas, Verdi's were a global phenomenon. For example, in the three years following its Rome premiere in 1853, *Il trovatore* received more than 200 separate productions around the world.

Along with the growing popularity of opera, concert halls proliferated across Europe. The capacities of the Hanover Square Rooms and the Leipzig Gewandhaus were in the high hundreds, but some of the newer halls could accommodate thousands – and they weren't all aristocrats. These new concert halls sold tickets at the door and, to the horror of some, a growing middle class was eager to buy them. In keeping with the need to fill larger halls, early-nineteenth-century concerts often involved considerable showmanship. Today we think of Beethoven's violin concerto as one of his most sublime works, its long first movement lyrical and rather slow by the standards of other famous concertos, followed by a second, still slower movement. But at its first performance in 1806, the soloist, Franz Clement, lightened the mood by playing a novelty piece of his own between these movements. What's more, he played it all on one string while holding the violin upside down.

Clara Schumann at the piano

Just as opera had its stars, now so did concert music, and high among them was another violinist, the Genoan virtuoso Niccolò Paganini, with a playing technique so remarkable that, like the blues guitarist Robert Johnson a century later, he was rumoured to be in league with the devil. The composer Liszt was a similar figure at the piano keyboard; indeed, he modelled himself to some degree on Paganini. His reputation as a showman created a Europe-wide craze for his concerts, with women fighting for pieces of his clothing and locks of his hair: 'Lisztomania', the poet Heinrich Heine called it. Along with Clara Schumann, a very different sort of musician, Liszt may be said to have invented the piano recital, that gladiatorial pitting of a solo player against a grand piano. As late as 1842, this was still a considerable novelty, and a critic in St Petersburg expressed astonishment that 'Liszt appeared alone on the stage throughout the entire concert . . . What conceit! What vanity! . . . And in such an immense hall!'

Schumann herself was not averse to showing off – like Liszt, she played in public from memory, which some regarded as a vulgar display – and to begin with she included her share of party pieces. Her early concerts were packed with flashy variations on popular operatic arias of the day, including a set of her own on the cavatina from Bellini's opera *Il pirata* (The Pirate). But as early as the mid-1830s, the teenage Clara was also including Bach fugues and Beethoven sonatas in her programs. In 1841, she wrote in her diary of her distaste for 'mechanical virtuosity': 'Concert pieces such as Henselt's etudes, fantasies by Thalberg, Liszt etc. have become completely repugnant to me'. Still, she was enough of a businesswoman to know she must offer audiences at least some of what they wanted. As she pointed out to Brahms, she wasn't giving concert tours for her own pleasure.

Too often Clara Schumann is portrayed as a victim, someone who was obliged to give up composition in order to have eight children, guard the fragile mental health of her composer husband Robert, and play public concerts so as to put food on the table. All of that is true, but as a pianist she was famous before she married Robert, and she was still giving concerts thirty-five years after his death. What she achieved in that role, transforming the nascent piano recital, was as important as the work of any of the individual composers she championed. Before her, concerts meant novelties and frivolities; by the time she retired from playing in public in 1891, they were serious affairs. Where once audiences had flocked to see and hear Liszt (who had given up concert life in 1847), now they came to see Clara Schumann and hear 'classical music'.

* * *

> The repertoire is limited to a small pool of works centring on the big instrumental compositions by the Viennese masters; everything else is more or less excluded. In particular, the works of young, living composers are all too often neglected.
>
> —Franz Brendel (1811–1868),
> German music critic

The nineteenth century was when the notion of classical music and musical canons took root, a literary tradition of great 'works' against which new composers might measure themselves, assuming they could get their music heard. Brendel's remark, made in 1850, is an apt description of the classical concert hall in the twentieth and twenty-first centuries, so it is interesting to note that old music seems to have been edging out the new almost from the start. Now that it was no longer the preserve of the aristocracy, classical music was now available to anyone with the necessary shilling to gain admission to a concert, and like many a paying punter, audiences wanted value for money, the tried-and-true music of the past offering a guarantee of quality. According to J. Peter Burkholder, writing on nineteenth-century European concert culture, approximately 80 per cent of the music performed in 1800 was by living composers, but in the three decades from 1850 the proportion had shrunk to 20 per cent.

This veneration of composers from the past had a knock-on effect for their successors, who saw themselves as heirs to Mozart and Beethoven. These composers might have been happy to receive commissions from wealthy patrons (composers still are) but, no longer servants, they now regarded themselves as independent freelancers, heroic artists addressing the whole of humanity – at least as much of humanity as could fit into a concert hall. Some of the new concert halls had the names of history's most celebrated composers carved into their walls, and as these halls grew in size, orchestras expanded to fill them. Once, orchestral music had been conducted by the principal violinist or (as in Haydn's case) by the composer at a keyboard, but these large orchestras, playing more elaborate works, had independent conductors – in some cases more 'heroic' as the composers themselves – whose role it was not only to coordinate performances but to shape the musical work with their charisma.

The public music critic was also born, as concert reviews in newspapers offered a new form of democratic engagement; given that the music itself was now often too technically demanding for audience members to play at home, at least you had an expert opinion to argue with the following morning. A loftier calling yet was that of the musicologist, making a surprisingly late entrance to Western music in the form of monographs on composers and their works. In 1837, A.B. Marx published four volumes on music theory, illustrated with examples from Beethoven's music. China had had musicologists in ancient times, but in Europe the idea that the study of music might be a science – *Musikwissenschaft* – was first stated in 1863 by Friedrich Chrysander. The eighteenth century had produced some historical writing about music, but this notion that it was a phenomenon that could be analysed and from which theories might be drawn was new, and with it came yet more attention to music's recent past. Older music by Handel and Bach was rediscovered, studied and published. Chrysander himself edited the keyboard works of the baroque composer François Couperin (1668–1733), assisted by Brahms; two French composers, Camille Saint-Saëns and Vincent d'Indy, did the same for the works of Jean-Philippe Rameau (1683–1764). And Beethoven's influence grew ever more pronounced. Berlioz felt it, writing at length about the composer and threatening violence to a French critic of the fifth symphony. Wagner felt it, conducting the ninth symphony and penning a treatise on the subject. Brahms was overwhelmed by it, delaying his own first symphony until he was nearly forty and then writing a tune in his finale that was clearly in thrall to Beethoven's 'Ode to Joy'. When this was pointed out to Brahms he is said to have snapped, 'Any fool can hear that.'

* * *

> I know nothing more beautiful than [Beethoven's] *Appassionata*, I could hear it every day. It is marvellous, unearthly music. Every time I hear these notes, I think with pride and perhaps childlike naivety, that it is wonderful what man can accomplish. But I cannot listen to music often, it affects my nerves. I want to say amiable stupidities and stroke the heads of the people who can create such beauty in such a filthy hell.
>
> —Vladimir Lenin (1870–1924) to Maxim Gorky

By the twentieth century, the pattern for Western art music seemed established. Most of it – great music to be sure – had been composed during the previous 200 years and written by European men, especially Austrians and Germans; newer music would have to fight its way past these titans to gain access to the concert hall. The already sizeable middle-class audience for it broadened significantly with the advent of recordings and radio, classical music in the home no longer a matter of owning a piano. By the middle of the twentieth century, this music, composed by the sons of tradesmen first for the aristocracy and later for the bourgeoisie, belonged to everyone.

In retrospect, the decades of the 1930s, '40s and '50s were probably classical music's heyday. Never were more symphony orchestras created than in the 1930s, the decade of the Great Depression. Many of them were radio orchestras, courtesy of the broadcasting companies that had sprung up in the 1920s, and their playing standards were high. Within a few years of its formation in 1930, the BBC Symphony Orchestra in London was widely considered the finest in Europe. Radios carried classical concerts into people's homes. Most homes had only one radio, so everyone in a household listened to the same program and, consequently, the audience for these concerts was huge. From 1937, the NBC Symphony Orchestra in New York, which boasted Arturo Toscanini as its conductor and paid the highest salaries of any orchestra in the USA, made weekly broadcasts – first on radio, then television – and they continued until 1954, when Toscanini retired and the orchestra was disbanded.

Classical music was considered important and improving, and the Depression created a demand for culture. When the Second World War began, it was a matter of honour and necessity for concerts to continue. The London Blitz? Nothing daunted, Myra Hess continued her lunchtime piano recitals of Bach and Beethoven at the National Gallery in Trafalgar Square, long after the paintings themselves had been shipped to locations in Wales. The firebombing of Berlin? Wilhelm Furtwängler conducted Beethoven and Brahms at the Philharmonie until the RAF bombed it at the start of 1944, whereupon they played on at the State Opera.

Some classical music became particularly well known – the pieces were referred to as 'popular classics' – in certain cases attracting lyricists to turn them into popular *songs*. Tchaikovsky's music, with its big tunes, was a sitting duck. In 1939, the Harry James Orchestra recorded 'Moon Love' with a young Frank Sinatra, its melody adapted from the slow movement of the Russian composer's fifth symphony; two years later the second theme of his sixth symphony became 'The Story of a Starry Night' for Ray Eberle with the Glenn Miller Orchestra, while Tony Martin sang 'Tonight We Love', cannibalised from the opening theme of the first piano concerto. Plundering the classics never really stopped: in 1963, the Swingle Singers released *Jazz Sébastien Bach*, their gently swung, eight-part renditions of Bach's instrumental music with bass and drums; Wendy Carlos's *Switched-On Bach* (1968) transferred some of that composer's keyboard and orchestral music to the synthesiser; and Waldo de los Ríos' *Sinfonias* (1970) took movements of symphonies by Mozart, Schubert, Brahms and others and added an easy-listening rhythm section. But while much of this appropriation was little more than kitsch, the sound of classical music – at least its later stages – had already been exported, wholesale, to a new genre in a new medium: the movies.

European composers had looked to the United States since the late nineteenth century. Between 1892 and 1895, Dvořák was director of the National Conservatory of Music in New York (he composed his ninth symphony, *From the New World*, in a house on East 17th Street); Mahler visited New York four times between 1907 and 1911, conducting productions at the Metropolitan Opera and many concerts with the New York Philharmonic; following the Russian Revolution, Rachmaninoff went to New York and reinvented himself as a concert pianist, touring the United States for the last twenty-five years of his life. Another Russian composer–pianist, Dimitri Tiomkin, also sought a new start in the United States (in 1928, Tiomkin gave the European premiere of Gershwin's piano concerto in Paris in the composer's presence); Max Steiner, godson of Richard Strauss and a pupil of Mahler, went to New York, not as a classical musician, but an orchestrator and music director, where he worked for more than a decade on Broadway shows. But from the early 1930s, with talking pictures in their infancy, Hollywood became a magnet for musicians, with Steiner and Tiomkin among those who quickly found work there. With the rise of fascism in Europe, they were joined by other Jewish composers, as well as actors, writers, directors and designers.

Because most early film music was provided by European emigres, its style was late-Romantic: Liszt, Tchaikovsky, Wagner and Strauss were audible influences on the music of Steiner (*King Kong*, *Little Women*, *Gone with the Wind*, *Casablanca*), Tiomkin (*Lost Horizon*, *It's a Wonderful Life*, *Duel in the Sun*), Erich Wolfgang Korngold (*The Adventures of Robin Hood*, *The Sea Wolf*, *King's Row*) and Franz Waxman (*Bride of Frankenstein*, *Captains Courageous*, *Rebecca*); and this style persisted, at least when a full orchestra was used on the soundtrack of a blockbuster. In John Williams's scores from the 1970s, while there may be a little less Wagner, there's plenty of Korngold and Steiner in addition to other twentieth-century composers: one detects, for instance, the influence of Stravinsky (*Jaws*), Holst and Walton (the early *Star Wars* films) and Prokofiev (*ET*). The influence of Stravinsky is paradoxical in that this composer, himself resident in Hollywood from 1941, could never find work in the film industry, despite the use of *The Rite of Spring* in Disney's *Fantasia* (1940).

Particularly in the years before television, film industries around the world flourished, led by their top studios, and they played an important role in the popularising of music. Broadway shows were made into Hollywood musicals and in some cases the other way round. *42nd Street* hit the screens in 1933, just six years after the first talking picture was released, but didn't become a stage musical until 1980. Outside the United States, the largest film industry was in India. Hindi cinema, later popularly known as Bollywood, began in the 1890s, and after its first talking picture in 1931, the primary genre was the musical. The scale of the popularity of Hindi musicals made stars not only of those on screen but also of the playback artists who provided their singing voices. Hollywood tried to keep secret the identity of someone like Marni Nixon, who dubbed the singing voices of Deborah Kerr in *The King and I*, Natalie Wood in *West Side Story* and Audrey Hepburn in *My Fair Lady*, but Bollywood celebrated Asha Bhosle and her ilk. Bhosle, who sang for her first film at the age of ten in 1943, was named history's biggest-selling recording artist by the *Guinness Book of Records* in 2011. Bigger, that is, than Bing Crosby, Elvis Presley and the Beatles.

With the advent of television, a number of Hollywood composers began to work in the new medium; Waxman's score for the 1957 film *Peyton Place* morphed easily enough into his theme music for the 1964 TV series of the same name, while Tiomkin's semi-specialisation as a composer for cowboy films made him a natural choice to write the theme for *Rawhide*. But music originally composed for the concert hall or opera house was also used in film and television. In *Brief Encounter* (David Lean, 1945), Celia Johnson and Trevor Howard's love affair was egged on by Eileen Joyce playing Rachmaninoff's second piano concerto, while few people who watched television in the 1950s would ever be able to shake the association of the overture to Rossini's opera *William Tell* with the long-running cowboy series *The Lone Ranger*.

For all that, the brief ubiquity of certain pieces of Western art music was already on the wane; the arrival of recordings, which had helped to popularise classical music, was also its slow undoing. Commercial recording changed everything (see Chapter Five), but it affected different sorts of music in different ways. Bearing in mind that early records, spinning at seventy-eight revolutions per minute, could only hold between three and five minutes of music per side, these discs were well suited to the early years of jazz and swing and the birth of the international hit song. Three-to-five-minute sides were never going to be much use for classical music. Even a short symphony would require two sides per movement. In 1904 the release of the first complete recording of an opera (Verdi's *Ernani*) by the Italian Gramophone Company occupied forty single-sided discs. With multi-disc sets of symphonies or operas, the individual records (each in its own paper cover) were presented in a large folder, rather like a photograph album, and the term 'album' stuck.

Notwithstanding the continued popular appeal of opera – especially in Italy – forty-disc albums were a luxury item. The real business was in 'singles' (including operatic excerpts), and this persisted into the 1950s and 1960s, as long-playing vinyl took over from albums of 78s, and thin, 7-inch-diameter discs spinning at 45 revolutions per minute became the new singles.

The recording age didn't diminish the fame of classical music's stars, but pop music and jazz were *created* by sound recording, even if they had diametrically opposed relationships to the medium. As an improvised form of music, jazz was arguably misrepresented by recordings. You listened to records of Charlie Parker or Betty Carter and heard a frozen moment, a unique performance of 'Ornithology' or 'The Way You Look Tonight', spontaneity being the whole point of jazz. If you went to hear either of these artists live and they performed the same tunes, you would expect a different approach; to borrow the title of one of Carter's albums, jazz was 'not about the melody' but about what the performer did with it. By contrast, pop-music fans, for whom the *ur*-text of a song was the 45-rpm single, could feel cheated if they attended a live concert and their favourite song did not resemble the version they already knew.

Sound recording made pop music in its many forms a global phenomenon, one capable of fomenting social as well as musical change. Records turned certain performers into national heroes. Egypt's Umm Kulthum is a prime example of a singer who continuously reinvented herself while inspiring little short of devotion in her native country and throughout the Arab world. She had a powerful and distinctive alto voice and could embody a song, sometimes in live performance for up to an hour; but there was more to her fame than just singing. For all her commercial success, Kulthum always carried a certain spiritual authority (her father, who had taught her to sing, had been an imam) and at times of national introspection – for example, after Egypt's defeat in the Six-Day War of 1967 – her recordings flooded Egyptian radio.

* * *

> No one can describe the extent of my pride when
> I went to Paris, stood in the middle of Europe,
> and raised my voice in the name of Egypt.
>
> —Umm Kulthum (1898–1975), Egyptian singer

Edith Piaf's place in the hearts of her French public mirrored Kulthum's in the Arab world. Again there was the distinctive voice, again the ability to put across a song as though from her very soul; but Piaf's story was one of poverty and misfortune:

she was abandoned by her mother, her daughter died in infancy, her great love (the boxer Marcel Cerdan) was killed in a plane crash on his way to meet her and, following her own injuries in a series of car accidents, she battled drug and alcohol addiction. If Kulthum represented Arab pride, Piaf stood for French resilience and survival. 'Je ne regrette rien,' she sang – I regret nothing – her charismatic defiance overriding doubts about her wartime years in Nazi-occupied Paris, where she was a favourite with German officers.

Kulthum and Piaf shared the burnished image that came with many a successful recording career, commercial success encouraging fascination with a performer's own story; the story, in turn, helping to sell records. In the case of Elvis Presley, the image outshone the musical fame, at least until after his death, so it is important to stress that, like Kulthum and Piaf, Presley had an immense musical gift; moreover, with that magnificent tenor voice (and the right training), he could have sung anything. What he did sing was a fusion of musical styles – African American blues plus what was still, in the 1950s, known as hillbilly music – while his hips swivelled, his hair flopped and his lip curled. Presley's first recordings, made in 1954 and 1955 at Memphis's Sun Studio, remain engagingly fresh, but in 1956 the entrepreneur 'Colonel' Tom Parker took the singer to RCA Victor, where he recorded 'Heartbreak Hotel' and 'Blue Suede Shoes' and history was created. If the voices of Umm Kulthum and Edith Piaf spoke, primarily, to Arab and French audiences, Presley's spoke to a generation. It is not much of an exaggeration to say that in

Western countries in general and the United States in particular, the advent of rock and roll in the late 1950s coincided with the invention of the modern teenager. Little Richard was more important musically and Chuck Berry in terms of songwriting, but Elvis had the voice and the hips and the hair and the lips; and, it's worth adding, he was white.

When Tom Parker took his protégé to RCA, he made him into a star. Presley's first single and first album each sold a million copies – RCA had never had a million-selling pop album before. 'Heartbreak Hotel', the single, and 'Blue Suede Shoes', the first track on the album, were written by professional songwriters – respectively, Mae Boren Axton and Tommy Durden, stalwarts of the Nashville country music scene, and rockabilly singer Carl Perkins – but structurally, both songs were blues: 'Heartbreak Hotel' is an eight-bar blues; 'Blue Suede Shoes' twelve bars. We can make too much of appropriation; you can't copyright a simple chord sequence, and anyway no one owns the copyright to eight- and twelve-bar blues. Still, it's hard to read RCA's sales figures from the late 1950s and beyond and not think of Blind Boy Fuller and his tin can.

In the twentieth century, because of recordings – and film and radio and television – music became a multinational industry, corporate executives making a lot of money from the work and ideas of those they so dismissively came to refer to as 'creatives'. The blues, country music and their offspring rock and roll; gospel and its secular counterpart soul; funk and R&B; rocksteady and reggae; Afrobeat and township jive;

metal and grunge; rap and the entire hip hop culture; C-pop and K-pop and J-pop: however mass manufactured some of these musical styles may now seem (and often are), they began on the street or in someone's garage. The ever-expanding niche categories of electronic dance music in the late twentieth and early twenty-first centuries – acid house, ambient dub, dark step, drone, tech trance, trip hop and a hundred more – can sometimes seem like the 'creatives' trying to keep the 'corporates' at bay.

Down the millennia, musicians have found a variety of ways to sell their work, from putting out the collecting tin, to seeking the patronage of princes and popes. Sometimes they were lucky, finding a busy street corner with a little extra room where passers-by might stop, or a cultured prince, genuinely enthusiastic about what his director of music might come up with next. There are still street musicians and still patrons of the arts, though they tend not to live in palaces, and during the twentieth century government funding of music (meagre or generous, depending upon the government) took over from the princes and the popes, while some composers found themselves on university faculties.

But when pop music became big business a lot of things changed, including artists' control over the nature of their work and, in the age of streaming services, the chances of even a successful musician being adequately paid.

4

MUSIC AND MODERNISM: REINVENTING THE ART FROM 1150 TO THE PRESENT

YOU ARE IN A CONCERT HALL at a piano recital. The performer comes on stage, acknowledges the applause, sits, lifts the lid of the instrument and waits . . . and waits . . . for four minutes and thirty-three seconds. Then the pianist stands, bows to the audience again, and leaves.

You have just sat through a performance of *4'33"*, composed by John Cage in 1952. The score, such as it is, consists of three movements, each marked 'tacet', which, to a musician, means 'don't play'. The Latin word literally means 'is silent', but in a concert hall, especially one in which audience members may be wondering what is going on (is the pianist ill or waiting for the lighting to change or about to get up and storm off?), there will never be silence. There will be shuffling, whispering, page-riffling, throat-clearing, and we will hear it all, because we seldom listen so hard as when we are waiting for music to start. To Cage, echoing the thirteenth-century Sufi philosopher

Abu al-Hasan al-Shushtari, all that was required to turn a randomly encountered sound into music was concentration.

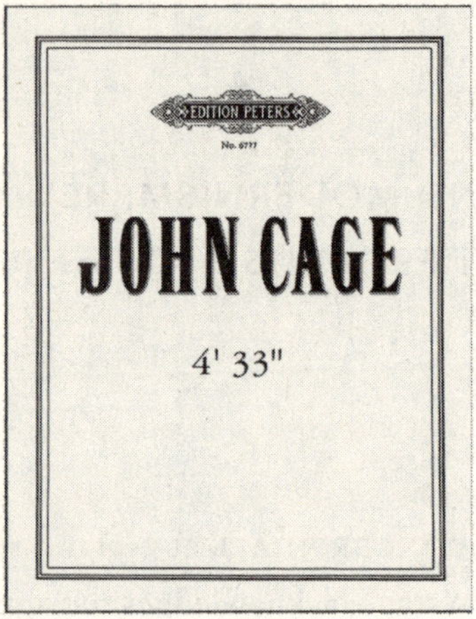

Cover of Cage's *4'33"*

* * *

> O sing unto the Lord a new song
>
> —Psalm 96

Modernism's agenda is to 'make it new', as the poet Ezra Pound urged in 1934. This is not just a matter of the psalmist's 'new song', but a whole new type of song. At its most extreme – and it doesn't get more extreme than *4'33"* – musical modernism asks us to reassess what music can be, and we may recognise that aim in much art from the first six decades of the twentieth century. In music, painting, sculpture and literature there was a rejection of Romanticism and a grab for what the art historian Robert Hughes called 'the shock of the new'. Artists such as Picasso, Matisse, Kandinsky and Mondrian, writers like Joyce, Eliot, Woolf and Gertrude Stein, composers including Stravinsky and Schoenberg, Bartók and Webern, Louis Armstrong, Duke Ellington and Mary Lou Williams: these are among the names we think of first. Following the Second World War, a second wave of what we might call 'high modernism' upped the ante, especially in music, as Boulez, Cage and Stockhausen attempted to wipe the slate clean of a musical past they associated with a kind of societal inertia. In jazz, the bebop of Charlie Parker, Dizzy Gillespie and Bud Powell attempted something similar; by the mid-1950s, rock and roll had arrived. All this music was consciously modern.

Throughout history there have been musicians who sang with distinctive voices or found more efficient or more impressive ways to play an instrument. They were influential; others heard and copied them, adding a lilt or a growl to their singing, a flourish to their playing, another string to their bow. The great sitar player Ravi Shankar, who had such a central role in the revival and popularisation of classical Hindustani music following India's independence in 1947, brought new approaches to the music's performance, duetting with other musicians and other instruments (jugalbandi) and forging a personal style of playing that included the creation of new ragas; he also collaborated with musicians from other genres and musical traditions, the likes of Yehudi Menuhin and Philip Glass. But he did not materially alter the way that Hindustani music operated and never set out to do so. He enriched the tradition; he didn't reinvent it.

The idea that you can tear up the music rule book and start again depends upon there having been a book in the first place. Because Western art music is a literary tradition as well as a musical one, it is written down, indexed, bound and shelved in libraries; because the music is not dependent upon memory and repetition to keep it alive, it can be rejected by a new generation of musicians who have found their own ways to do things. The older music will remain safely on its shelf and may be taken down for a performance whenever desired, and the next generation is free to go its own way. It is the same with recorded music. Bebop had no duty of care to Duke Ellington or Count Basie, because their recordings lived on; try as it might, punk couldn't destroy progressive rock, it could only put up two musical fingers at it.

Paradoxically, modernism is itself a tradition in Western music dating back at least to the middle of the twelfth century, and it is this tradition that has encouraged some musicologists to view the history of Western music as a matter of progress. The approach gives pride of place to those musicians who wrought material change in composition, elevating the reputations of Monteverdi, Haydn, Beethoven, Berlioz, Wagner, Debussy, Stravinsky, Schoenberg and so on. Nothing wrong with that, except that it leaves out the likes of Bach, Mozart, Mendelssohn, Brahms and Elgar. No one today would think of the composers on that second list as modernists, but only those of an irredeemably ideological bent would argue they weren't among Europe's greatest musical minds.

We must always be careful not to confuse modernism with originality, which is ultimately more important. Music may be both modernist and original, but it is equally possible to be highly original and relatively conservative.

Tchaikovsky's Piano Concerto No 1 in B flat minor is a good example of the latter. Long before it became one of those 1940s pop songs, the big tune at the start of the concerto was famous. It was also, in its proper setting, a very original moment.

The first movements of nineteenth-century concertos tended to follow a general pattern that had evolved in the eighteenth century as a musical corollary to Enlightenment reason and rhetoric. The music would propose a first theme or subject in the tonic (or home key); then, once established, it would be followed by a contrasting theme, usually in the dominant key (a fifth higher) – on the one hand this, but on the other hand that. There followed a short or extended section in which the two themes or fragments of them were 'debated', usually involving modulation to more distant keys, before a recapitulation of the original theme and a safe and often triumphant landing back in the home key. That's a simplification, but it's broadly true of most Classical and Romantic first movements; it was known as 'sonata form'.

Tchaikovsky's piano concerto does not follow this pattern. For one thing, while the home key of this concerto is B flat minor, that famous opening theme is in D flat major. Then there's the role of the solo piano. By 1875, when the piece was written (it was revised in 1888), concerto soloists were accustomed to playing the hero, but this concerto sets out with the piano as accompanist: the big tune is given to the strings while the soloist just plays chords, up and down the keyboard. Then comes a wholly unexpected cadenza. Such moments of maximum display for the soloist (the orchestra falling silent) traditionally happened just before the end of a movement, not a few minutes after the start.

So far, then, so original; but the most surprising aspect of this concerto is what Tchaikovsky does next with this famous theme. He does nothing. Not usually one to abandon a good tune when he can use it again and again, here he does just that. The opening theme – the bit that everyone knows and that made the concerto into a popular classic – is not put through its paces in a development section and neither does it return at the end in a triumphant recapitulation; it simply vanishes. It's fair to say that no previous piano concerto had ever quite done what Tchaikovsky's first did, but for all its unconventionality, it was recognisably a Romantic piano concerto, belonging in the same company as those by Liszt and Brahms. It was not modernist.

In Ruth Crawford Seeger's String Quartet, something like the opposite situation obtains. The prevailing style and intent of the music is high twentieth-century modernist, and it isn't hard to find precursors and models in the music of Schoenberg and Bartók. Indeed, the first two movements of Crawford Seeger's quartet seem to owe much to the *Lyric Suite* of Alban Berg, composed just five years earlier. Crawford Seeger had met Berg in Europe while she was writing her quartet. To its midpoint, then, this is modernist music with precedent. Then comes the third movement, 'Andante', as though from nowhere.

At its outset, it also briefly resembles the *Lyric Suite*'s fourth movement, with its dark hues and slow semitonal trills, but this time the composer pays Berg just a glancing nod. Crawford Seeger's 'Andante' slowly pulses with an expanding harmonic palette, as clusters of notes ascend ever higher, and it also appears to breathe.

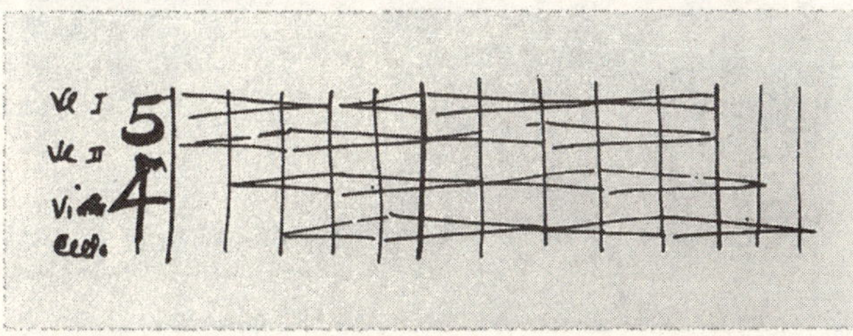

A diagrammatic illustration in Crawford Seeger's own hand of the 'heterophony of dynamics' in the 'Andante' of her *String Quartet* (1931)

'The underlying plan,' the composer wrote in her own analysis of this movement, 'is heterophony of dynamics – a sort of counterpoint of crescendi and diminuendi . . . No high point in the crescendo in any one instrument coincides with the high point in any other instrument.'

The four players form a single throbbing organism, a blended sonority in which the cello often plays higher notes than the viola and the first violin is sometimes given the lowest notes of all. The climax is shattering and violent, before the music falls away to silence. There really was nothing like this movement before it. The music is original *and* modernist, and like all the best modernism it still packs a punch.

Ludwig and Malvina Schnorr von Carolsfeld in the premiere of *Tristan und Isolde* in 1865

Years, even centuries, later, great music can maintain its modernity. The blistering heat of Jimi Hendrix's guitar and Charlie Parker's alto sax, and the torrent of spontaneous invention that comes from both; the explosion of glitter that signals the start of Pierre Boulez's *Le Marteau sans maître*; the blink-and-you've-missed-it brevity of Anton Webern's *Bagatelles* for string quartet (six pieces together lasting three-and-a-half minutes); the pile-up of dissonance at the climax of the 'Adagio' from Mahler's unfinished tenth symphony; the harmonic ambiguity at the opening of Wagner's *Tristan und Isolde*; the abruptly shifting metres in the finale of Beethoven's final piano sonata and the unstoppable, jagged counterpoint of the *Grosse Fuge*; the heightened dramatic speech of Monteverdi's operas; the muscular syncopation of Léonin's *Viderunt omnes* at Notre-Dame de Paris 800 years ago: it all continues to challenge comfortable listening, bringing jolts and surprises.

First production of *The Rite of Spring*, Paris, 1913

It's true that overfamiliarity can reduce the impact of a once startling piece. Cage's *4'33"* loses its effectiveness in front of an audience that knows what's coming – and what isn't coming – while *The Rite of Spring*, which made its composer Stravinsky famous after the riot prompted by its premiere in 1913, has become something of an orchestral party piece. But the score of *4'33"*, published by the 200-year-old family firm Edition Peters, retains a degree of iconoclasm – Peters published Bach, Haydn, Beethoven and Chopin, and Cage's page of music, inside the same pale green cover, is blank. And in a great performance, the savagery of *The Rite* may still upset some audience members; as recently as the 1980s, disgruntled patrons were spotted leaving the concert hall of the Sydney Opera House mid-performance.

* * *

> I am a feather on the breath of God.
>
> — Hildegard of Bingen (1098–1179), German composer, writer and Benedictine abbess

Hildegard probably didn't think she was being modern, let alone modernist, as she sketched the endlessly proliferating melodic line of *O ecclesia oculi tui* (in praise of St Ursula and her 11,000 virgins), but there were no real precedents for what she did at her Rhineland monasteries. It possibly helped, as it would help Haydn six centuries later, that Hildegard was cut off from the world. Her isolation enabled her to ignore the strictures demanded by the Cistercian Order, which aimed to keep melodic lines within a narrow span and melismatic singing (more than one note to a syllable) to a minimum. The problem as they saw it was wide-ranging melodies and long melismas distracting from the meaning of the words (the Cistercians also disapproved of illuminated manuscripts). Hildegard's melodies soared and wheeled like her famous feather on the breath of God, often spanning as much as two octaves (the Cistercians felt a perfect fourth was quite wide enough), and some of her melismas included twenty or more notes.

One of history's constants when it comes to musical innovation is some critic waiting to carp and cavil. While Hildegard was composing her sequences on the Rhine and Léonin was writing his organa in Paris, across the English Channel a Cistercian monk at Rievaulx Abbey in Yorkshire was writing a treatise entitled *Speculum caritatis* (The Mirror of Love), including a chapter on 'The Vain Pleasure of the Ears' in which he railed at vocal excess.

> One sings bass, another alto, yet another soprano. Yet another adds decorations and trills all up and down the melody. The voice strains at one point, and fades the next. It speeds up, then slows down making all sorts of noises. Shameful though it is to admit it, sometimes the voice sounds like the whinnying of horses; sometimes, spurning manliness, it is reduced to feminine shrillness.
>
> —Aelred of Rievaulx (1110–1167),
> English Cistercian abbot

Religious and political attempts to curb artistic freedom are as old as religion, politics and art, and artists continue to run up against censorship – sometimes placing them in physical danger – when they break what passes for rules. Hildegard, of course, was not creating art; she was expressing devotion to her God. The novelty of Hildegard's music was a function of her original mind, and it was the same with the Notre-Dame composers.

Yet these musicians, while often sequestered from society, were still part of the world of ideas, and the twelfth century in Europe was a renaissance before the Renaissance, in painting, architecture and music, in politics, science and theology. As in the late fifteenth and sixteenth centuries (and in the so-called Carolingian Renaissance of the eighth and ninth centuries), Greek and Roman literature was rediscovered and translated, and there was renewed interest in Greek science, now with Arabic additions; the Islamic influence was at its height on the Iberian Peninsula, bringing with it new inventions (paper in 1110). Most noticeably, a pointed style of architecture that would become known as Gothic began to dominate the European landscape, with giant cathedrals and abbeys springing up at a remarkable rate. These buildings dwarfed the tiny dwellings of the ordinary people who built them, and that was half the idea: to overwhelm Christendom with the fear of God. If you stepped into one of these buildings, such as Notre-Dame de Paris, begun in 1163, the lines of the architecture guided your eye up and up – to the high vaulted ceiling and to heaven beyond. All that was needed now was some suitably impressive sound to fill that enormous space. Enter Léonin and Pérotin with their rhythmically dynamic, multi-voiced organa and the beginnings of harmony.

Even without the vastness of Notre-Dame's interior, sunshine streaming through the high stained glass to lighten our darkness below, there is something thrillingly theatrical about that music, and it is possible that the theological imperatives that lay behind it, and the need to respond with music that was suitably dazzling, led these composers to innovate. But if we think of Notre-Dame as a theatre (which at some level it certainly was), we can situate Léonin and Pérotin at the start of a European tradition, one in which the need for drama brings musical change.

* * *

> See the music, listen to the theatre!
>
> —Luciano Berio (1925–2003),
> Italian composer

Opera is the ultimate multimedia art, a traditional form of which has existed in China since the time of the Notre-Dame composers. Today there are more than 300 distinct varieties of 'Chinese opera' associated with different geographical regions, layers of society and dialects. Xiqu, to use the correct term, brings together speech and mime, song and instrumental music, dance, acrobatics, slapstick, costume and makeup. Staging is simple – few props and no scenery – but the visual side of xiqu is important because it is through costume, makeup and elaborate, formalised gesture that character is established and developed. The vocalisation straddles speech and song, the speech always stylised, exaggerated and song-like, while the actual songs are based on traditional tunes, sometimes greatly ornamented, but not specially composed. Xiqu is a hybrid art, whereas Western opera, though driven by a dramatic impulse, was primarily a musical form.

Claudio Monteverdi's *L'Orfeo* was not the first opera in Europe – it wasn't even the first opera about Orpheus – but it remains a touchstone when we speak of the origins of the form, in part because of the way in which the music embodies and conveys the drama. There had been musical theatre in Europe since at least the Middle Ages. Hildegard, indeed, composed a morality play with music, *Ordo Virtutum* (The Order of the Virtues), around 1150. But in the sixteenth century, the scholars of the Florentine Camerata looked to ancient Greek theatre – at least their idea of it – as a model for a new approach to sung drama with continuous music. In particular, the Florentines believed that the Greeks had a sung style of speech which they called *stile recitativo*, and it was this spoken music founded on the rhythms of natural speech that Monteverdi employed with such power, along with a freer approach to dissonance than his Renaissance forebears. Sixteenth-century composers had tended to set up moments of harmonic tension, preparing the way for a dissonance, then resolving it. Monteverdi, who was after dramatic impact, was more inclined to use dissonance to take his listeners by surprise. Of course there was a critic, Giovanni Maria Artusi, to complain about it in his treatise, *On the Imperfections of Modern Music*.

In *L'Orfeo* music becomes drama and drama music. When Orpheus wishes to bring the dead Eurydice back from Hades, he must first persuade the psychopomp Charon to ferry him across the river Styx. So he sings him a flattering song, 'Possente spirto e formidabil nume' ('Mighty spirit and formidable god'), the flattery not only in the words but also in the lavish ornamentation of the musical line, which Monteverdi went to the trouble of writing out in full. Singers of this period were expected to add their own embellishments, but for this important dramatic moment the composer was leaving nothing to chance. Charon is flattered all right, but not about to grant Orpheus his ride, so Orpheus sings one more verse, this time unadorned, boring the ferryman to sleep before making off with his boat.

L'Orfeo was composed while Monteverdi was in the employ of Vincenzo Gonzaga, Duke of Mantua (the painter Rubens was also on staff) and, for all its historical significance, it received just two performances at the court and might have disappeared altogether but for the printed score commissioned by the Duke as a memento of the occasion.

From 1613, Monteverdi was in Venice as maestro at St Mark's Basilica, where, in addition to composing liturgical music, he also produced his final and perhaps finest books of madrigals, and more operas, alas lost. Then, in 1631, he took the tonsure and the following year was admitted as a priest. He was sixty-five, a good age for the seventeenth century, and seems to have all but retired from music. But five years later Venice opened Europe's first public opera house, the Teatro San Cassiano, and Monteverdi began to compose again. We only have two of the three operas he wrote in old age, but the last of them contains an example of something really only opera can achieve.

L'incoronazione di Poppea (The Coronation of Poppaea), composed in 1643, concerns the marriage of two of ancient Rome's more monstrous figures, the emperor Nero and his mistress Poppaea Sabina. Which of them had the idea to murder Nero's mother depends upon which historian you believe; likewise the decision to banish and later murder Nero's wife, so Poppaea could become empress (after she'd divorced her second husband, whom she'd only married to get close to Nero). But it was probably Poppaea's idea to have Nero's adviser, Seneca, put to death. At any rate the opera ends with this odious couple singing 'Pur ti miro', a steamy love duet in which the two high voices trade erotically charged harmonic suspensions with each other on the bed of a repeating bass line, creating what Richard Taruskin memorably called a 'dissonant friction'. There's no doubt that this music is a representation of sex but, gorgeous as it is, there is also something horrible about it, particularly bearing in mind that a couple of years after their wedding the historical Nero is said to have kicked the pregnant Poppaea to death (a seventeenth-century Venetian audience would have known this). Monteverdi didn't compose 'Pur ti miro' – the number was added for a revival a few years after his death – but, whoever was responsible, it's quite a moment. The music is making us feel something we know we should not, and we find ourselves complicit in the sordid world of these people.

Because the music of an opera, however tied to its drama, is also separate from it, this is an art form ripe for ambiguity. The words can be telling us one thing, the music another – even the opposite. In the ensembles of Mozart's operas, we might hear four or more voices simultaneously expressing individual and contradictory points of view, something that can only happen because the words are being sung (were they being spoken, we would hear a confused hubbub). In Wagner's operas, the orchestra often moves at a different rate to the musical exchanges on stage, bringing back themes and fragments of themes that provide context for what is being sung, and sometimes providing commentary. Wagner called these themes 'leitmotifs' – guiding themes – and they provided not only commentary but structure.

From Monteverdi's time through to the early nineteenth-century *bel canto* operas of Bellini and Donizetti, opera had oscillated between recitatives (speech-like singing) and arias (songs – including duets, trios and larger ensembles, right up to chorus numbers), resulting in a stylised art in which, often enough, the drama was advanced in the recitatives, before everything stopped for a song. One of Wagner's innovations was to do away with this stop-start structure in favour of a continuous narrative flow, and his leitmotifs were the pillars that supported this more cinematic approach. With the advent of talking pictures in the late 1920s, film composers quickly learnt the technique. In John Williams's *Stars Wars* music, the leitmotifs are flashing neon.

Wagner's modernism was not merely structural. It was everywhere, including his use of the orchestration. Orchestral flexibility may not be what we think of first with *The Ring of the Nibelung*; it's the big set pieces we remember: the entry of the gods into Valhalla, the ride of the Valkyries, Siegfried's funeral march. Yet these four long nights in the theatre consist mostly of domestic conversations between father and daughter, husband and wife, brother and sister, and a great deal of the orchestration is matching chamber music, resourceful, detailed and intimate. There is also striking use of individual instruments such as the dark-toned bass clarinet, both in a solo role and as a mainstay of the woodwind writing. Wagner was not the first composer to use the instrument in opera, but no one else made such consistent or effective use of it.

However, Wagner's greatest musical achievement – again at the service of continuous drama – was his use of ever-evolving chromatic harmony. What does chromaticism mean? You could say that it's the opposite of diatonicism. A diatonic scale, remember, is C major or D minor or the Lydian mode: any scale of seven notes leading to a repetition of the first note an octave higher, the intervals between the eight notes consisting of five whole tones and two semitones. A chromatic scale uses all twelve possible pitches, and chromatic harmony, while underpinned by tonality, employs a hefty admixture of chromatic notes to muddy the waters. So, in the first four bars of Wagner's opera *Tristan und Isolde* (1857–59), the opening phrase of the prelude contains eight different pitches, while the second phrase adds the other four that make up a chromatic scale; moreover, it's a matter of debate what key the music is in. Four hours later, at the very end of the opera, it will turn out to have been B major. That's a long wait to discover the home key.

Wagner did not invent chromaticism. Bach's music is full of chromatic passages, though he seldom abandons his listener without a compass, and in the finale of Mozart's Symphony No 40 in G minor, there is a moment where the music is derailed by a brief passage that sounds each of the twelve chromatic pitches one after the other, but that's a kind of joke. Wagner's music often leaves us in harmonic limbo, and he was seldom joking.

Chromatic harmony suited the free-flowing form of *Tristan und Isolde*, and it was the very lifeblood of the two lovers.

Tristan and Isolde's love is illicit. Isolde is betrothed to the Cornish King Mark, and she and Tristan must keep their mutual passion hidden. They do not find this easy. During their long love duet in the second act, they submerge themselves in each other to the point of switching names as together they yearn for oblivion, which might be orgasm or death – or, as it turns out, both. After half an hour of passionate chromaticism – musical sex, again – the duet is evidently building to its climax, a harmonic homecoming, when suddenly King Mark barges in with Western harmony's most brutal instance of coitus interruptus. Now we must all wait until the end of the third and final act for Isolde's famous *Liebestod* – her 'love-death' – in which, in the absence of the now-dead Tristan, she gives a solo reprise of the duet and, all on her own, reaches that long-delayed climax, waves of B major breaking over her.

It is possible Wagner would have come up with his highly personal approach to chromatic harmony anyway, but it was surely putting the story of Tristan and Isolde on stage that led him to it in this particular manner. Operas tend to change composers. The dramatic imperative, the need to tell a story, to communicate dialogue to an audience: these are useful distractions, and artists are most themselves when they are least self-conscious.

* * *

> I was guided by no system whatever in *Le Sacre du printemps* [The Rite of Spring] . . . I had only my ears to help me. I heard and I wrote what I heard. I am the vessel through which *Le Sacre* passed.
>
> —Igor Stravinsky (1882–1971), Russian composer

Igor Stravinsky's first ballet score for Sergei Diaghilev's Ballets Russes was *The Firebird* in 1910, the 28-year-old composer drawing on his recent studies with Rimsky-Korsakov and his knowledge of Tchaikovsky's ballets *Swan Lake* and *The Sleeping Beauty* to create a glittering fairy-tale in sound, albeit full of original touches and hints at what might be around the corner. But the hints prepared no one for what Stravinsky did next. A stylistic chasm exists between *The Firebird* and *The Rite of Spring*, most obviously in the matter of rhythm but also harmony and orchestration – the glitter had gone, and yet only three years (and *Petrushka*) had intervened.

As with Monteverdi and Wagner, it was the subject of *The Rite of Spring* – a sacrificial virgin dancing herself to death in pagan Russia – that led Stravinsky to its sound. The score's most radical feature was its use of rhythm to drive the music. Often there is no harmonic change at all, the composer simply repeating a single dense chord for bars on end with unpredictable accents. The savagery may strike today's listeners with less force than it did its first audience, but Stravinsky's achievement seems as impressive as ever – more impressive, in a way, now some of the piece's notoriety has faded. *The Rite* is full of folk melodies from Lithuania and Russia and the chords, dense with pitches but widely spaced, are fabulously pungent (Stravinsky's chords would remain an inimitable feature of his music). The symphonic unity of *The Rite*, which Ravel noticed at the time (though hardly anyone else did), is a function of all this – the melodies, the chords and the rich, woody, brassy, drummy timbre – but above all it is because of Stravinsky's use of rhythm.

Composing the final 'Sacrificial Dance', Stravinsky found that notation was letting him down. He could play the music on his upright piano but could not think how to write it. This is because he was, in effect, coming at the music from the opposite direction to all Western composers before him.

The 'Sacrificial Dance' is built of tiny rhythmic cells, Stravinsky working like a mosaicist, with bricks of varying shapes and sizes: a cell of three semiquavers, a cell of two semiquavers, two cells of three, one of four, one of two, two more of three; some of the semiquaver beats are notes and some are rests. The music, which is loud and fast, is completely unstable, convulsing violently, and it was never going to fit into familiar metres of 3/4 or 4/4. Eventually, Stravinsky wrote it down the way it sounded, changing the metre from bar to bar: 3/16, 2/16, 3/16, 3/16, 2/8, 2/16, 3/16 and so on. There had been nothing like this in Western music.

* * *

> Where a host of others have continued to stammer and to pontificate, to chatter and to prejudge, to simper and to haggle, to rage, to threaten, to mock and to torpedo, Stravinsky has simply *acted*.
>
> —Pierre Boulez (1925–2016),
> French composer and conductor

Early in the twentieth century, Stravinsky and Arnold Schoenberg came to seem like the major figures of musical modernism, not least because of their ability to stir audiences to violent responses. On 31 March 1913, two months before the disturbance that greeted *The Rite of Spring* in Paris, there was fisticuffs at Vienna's Musikverein for a concert conducted by Schoenberg. It wasn't Schoenberg's music that caused the violence but a pair of orchestral songs by his pupil Alban Berg to aphoristic poems by Peter Altenberg. Amid the din of audience members whistling their disapproval, the concert organiser slapped a patron. Oscar Straus, the composer of operettas such as *The Chocolate Soldier*, was present and judged the slap the most harmonious sound of the night.

To modern ears, it is hard to hear what the fuss was about. Berg's *Altenberg Lieder* are characterised by lyrical vocal lines above luminous skeins of orchestral sound. Certainly this music is far from the relentless pounding of *The Rite of Spring* or even the shattering funeral march from Anton Webern's Six Pieces for Orchestra, played first on the Musikverein program. Perhaps, by this point in the evening, the audience had simply had enough.

It is worth pointing out here that modernist music doesn't have to be rebarbative. Debussy's *Prélude à l'après-midi d'un faune*, which Pierre Boulez judged the birth of modern music, had to be encored at its first performance in 1894. Debussy's radicalism was in ridding his music of the goal-orientated harmonic structures of 200 years of European music: all that sonata form, all that strife, all that homecoming. For Debussy, harmony could be colour rather than structure. 'Why should I modulate?' he asked.

In a way, Schoenberg was the most traditional of the early-twentieth-century modernists, for his music never abandoned its Germanic roots. As a teacher, he showed his students examples from Bach, Beethoven, Schubert and Brahms, and one senses those composers' presence in Schoenberg's own music, in the counterpoint, the rigorous working out of motifs, the long lines. His music's modernity, which is to do with the abandoning of tonality, was also a matter of evolution, rather than revolution. Schoenberg believed that he was simply taking the ramped-up chromatic harmony of a work such as *Tristan und Isolde* to its logical conclusion. In *Tristan* there had been passages in which it was impossible to be certain of the key; very well, then, let's do away with keys altogether! The moment at which Schoenberg leaves tonality behind comes in the final movement of his second string quartet (1908), when a soprano voice sings words by the German expressionist poet Stefan George: 'Ich fühle luft von anderem planeten' – 'I feel the air from another planet'.

* * *

> Only a psychiatrist can help Schoenberg now . . .
> He'd be better off shovelling snow than scribbling on manuscript paper.
>
> —Richard Strauss (1864–1949),
> German composer, writing to Alma Mahler

It may have been a logical step for Schoenberg, but it was a step too far for many of his listeners and even for some of Schoenberg's composer colleagues who had been with him to this point.

Schoenberg and his pupils, Berg and Webern, styled themselves the second Viennese school (the first Viennese school having been Haydn, Mozart and Beethoven), and the music they composed from around 1908 until the mid-1920s is usually described as 'atonal'. It's a poor label, even if absence of tonality was the composers' aim. In contrast to most of the world's traditional music with its drone as a tonal centre; in contrast to the pentatonic scales of East Asia, the ragas of India, the Persian dastgahs and Arabic maqams; in contrast to the preceding 800 years of Western art music; and in contrast to every popular song of every culture on earth, before and since: the music of the second Viennese school sought to do away with the hierarchy of pitch. There would be no note more important than another. This was the twentieth century, the world of Einstein not Newton, and the gravitational pull to the home key would be replaced by one in which all twelve pitches were relative only to each other.

Except that Einstein's theory of relativity didn't render gravity obsolete, and human ears refused to stop working as they always had. Atonality might have been Schoenberg's aim – the complete avoidance of keys – but the human ear will always seek and usually find a tonal centre. Even in Webern's tiny *Bagatelles* for string quartet, composed in 1913, which are so short precisely because the composer felt that every time he had sounded each of the twelve pitches, the piece must be over; even in *this* music the ear latches on to some pitches more than others. We can't help ourselves. And yet what Webern had begun to sense while writing this music was the germ of a system that over the next decades would come to dominate Western composition.

The composers of atonal music faced a crisis, because they had lost their principal means of structuring a musical work. Harmonic dissonance had been part of the Western composer's toolbox since medieval times, and crucial since the Renaissance; it was how a composer created tension and release. But if you didn't have a home key lurking in the background, if you had junked musical gravity and your pitches were floating free, then dissonance had no frame of reference; if one note was no more important than another, then everything was dissonant and nothing was. Without a home key, how could you even end a piece?

When Webern had sensed that each of his *Bagatelles* was over after he had sounded all twelve tones, he'd been on to something. Building on Webern's hunch, Schoenberg discovered that you could order the notes to write yourself a new rule book. Twelve-tone or serial music formed the pitches into strips – twelve-tone rows – and, once fixed, the row became a piece's DNA. Now, in theory, no one pitch could dominate because it couldn't be repeated until the other eleven had been sounded. You could use the rows forwards or backwards or upside down, but the structure remained, and the potential chaos of free atonality was averted, in the composer's mind at least.

From the early 1930s many young composers found themselves drawn to twelve-tone composition. Coincidentally, this was the moment in history at which the classical repertoire was reaching its widest listenership ever, with new orchestras springing up around the world, and radios and gramophones in most homes. Along with the great names of the past, living composers such as Sibelius and Rachmaninoff, their music rooted in tonality, enjoyed widespread popularity. In this environment, modernism, especially twelve-tone modernism, was, for audiences, a niche enthusiasm.

A more popular invention of the 1930s was big band swing,

and throughout the Second World War swing music and popular classics continued to dominate the air waves. But in the late 1940s, musical modernism got a new wind. It affected jazz as much as classical music, and in much the same way.

The degree to which twelve-tone composition caught on among composers was remarkable. There were those who preferred to take a leaf out of Stravinsky's book or plough their own furrow or simply pretend the twentieth century wasn't happening, but for many composers – not only in Europe, but in North and South America, in Asia and Australasia – Schoenberg's discovery slowly and inexorably became a lingua franca. That it was a technique, rather than a style, probably helped it become international, although in time it became a style too among less-talented composers who viewed the technique as a passport to sophistication, and whose 'plinks' and 'plonks' infuriated audiences, giving all twelve-tone music a bad name.

* * *

> You goddamn sissy . . . stand up and use your ears like a man!
>
> —Charles Ives (1874–1954), American composer, to an audience member in 1931

It was Webern more than Schoenberg who became the great exemplar for composers of the post-war generation, and Debussy more than Stravinsky. What young composers such as Boulez, Stockhausen and Luigi Nono took from Webern was the organisation of pitch and other elements of their music, but also, and more importantly, a kind of fragmentation, a splintering of melodic lines into individual notes across many octaves – the plinks and plonks of popular derision. From Debussy came the confirmation that a musical composition need not be a journey with a goal, but might consist of a series of moments. Some remarkably beautiful music came from this period – Stockhausen's *Kreuzspiel* (1951), Nono's *Il canto sospeso* (1956) – music of great delicacy and poise as well as sometimes brutal power, but the audience for it remained small.

In jazz, where the big bands of Benny Goodman and Duke Ellington, Count Basie and Artie Shaw had been the popular music of their day, the new style of bebop now baffled many listeners as much as the music of the classical avant-garde. There was an element of fragmentation in the melodic lines of Charlie Parker and Dizzy Gillespie that matched that of the post-Webern composers, and there was a frenzy too. This was intense music for listening to in small clubs; chamber jazz. What you couldn't do was dance to it.

Not all music is for everyone; probably no music is. Throughout history certain sorts of composition were only heard by the elites of society: the various forms of court music in ancient China and Korea; the hymns of Hildegard; the symphonies Haydn composed at Esterháza. Also, there was music that simply had less mass appeal: Bach's *Art of Fugue*; the late string quartets of Beethoven; the songs of Hugo Wolf. Perhaps the music of Boulez and Stockhausen and Nono was like this;

perhaps this is also where we file bebop. And yet, as Elisabeth Lutyens found, atonal and serial music came into its own in the cinema and not just for horror movies, while bebop provided the soundtrack to many a film noir. In some cases the cinema audiences must have been the same people inclined to storm out of a concert containing atonal music, people who would never have ventured near a jazz club.

* * *

> Certainly one of the aspects of modernism that interested me as a young person was that it made people angry. I remember, for instance, when Dimitri Mitropoulos played my old *Holiday Overture* . . . and we went out in Carnegie Hall to take a bow together, he pointed to the audience and said 'Those are our enemies'. That was something that, as a young person, impressed me.
>
> —Elliott Carter (1908–2012),
> American composer

One aspect of modernism that has been a historical mainstay is a temptation on the part of musicians to rough up their work, to make it in some way abrasive. Part of this was the appropriation by composers of vernacular music. Stravinsky had found his folk tunes for *The Rite of Spring* in a book, but his Hungarian contemporary Béla Bartók collected songs and dances, allowing their modes and rhythms to affect his own writing and bringing in the sound – one might almost say the flavour – of the music. In 1931, Bartók wrote that 'peasant music . . . simple, sometimes primitive' was never 'trivial'. Any composer 'in search of new ways cannot be led by a better master'. Accordingly, Bartók's string players are often asked to play roughly, and his pianists – including those who tackle his first piano concerto – must bring not only a fiercely honed classical technique, but also their fists. Amid movements with innocuous titles such as 'Allegro', 'Allegretto' and 'Andante' are 'Allegro barbaro', 'With Drums and Pipes', 'Swineherd's Dance' and 'Bear Dance'.

The use of folkloric material in classical works was hardly new. One hundred and fifty years before Bartók, Haydn had composed a bear dance of his own at the end of his first *Paris* symphony (No 82 in C), and there are several instances in his string quartets and symphonies of drones conjuring the sounds of bagpipes or hurdy-gurdies. There are folk tunes in the repertoire of Japanese gagaku and traditional elements in the court songs of African griots: the tendency on the part of trained professionals to draw on vernacular tunes and techniques is universal. Even in this context, however, Bartók's assertion that traditional music is a path to modernism is striking and an aspect of the modernist musician's desire to strip away sophistication in the name of 'progress'.

This wasn't just a matter of drawing on folk music. Sometimes it was the adoption of an insistent phrase relentlessly pursued, as in *The Rite of Spring*; Beethoven's fifth symphony might be another example, built as it was from the rhythm of its famous four-note opening, a motif that never really goes away. The nineteenth-century essayist John Ruskin had a point when he wrote that Beethoven's music reminded him of 'the upsettings of bags of nails'. Beethoven took music in such a radical direction that his biggest fan, the composer Berlioz, would write in a letter to his father that 'this is no longer music but a new art'. Much the same was said at the start of the twentieth century about the advent of jazz, a modernist music if ever there was one.

* * *

> Jazz speaks for life. The Blues tell the story of
> life's difficulties, and if you think for a moment,
> you will realize that they take the hardest realities
> of life and put them into music, only to come
> out with some new hope or sense of triumph.
> This is triumphant music.
>
> —Martin Luther King Jr (1929–1968),
> American Baptist minister and
> civil rights leader

New Orleans, Louisiana had long been a musical melting pot (and every other sort of melting pot too), the city's brass bands dating back to the beginning of the nineteenth century, along with classical orchestras and opera companies. But after the American Civil War, cheap second-hand cornets and trombones, clarinets and drums – the instruments of army marching bands – were everywhere. Along with those plantation staples – the banjo, washboard and washtub bass – military castoffs contributed to the pool of instruments from which early jazz bands drew their basic line-up.

Buddy Bolden (standing, second from left) with his band, c. 1905

Given that its origins coincided with those of sound recording, it is frustrating that the first jazz we can hear is as late as 1917, when the Original Dixieland Jass (*sic*) Band recorded 'Livery Stable Blues', complete with animal sounds – a whinnying cornet and a crowing clarinet. It's fine playing and an important recording, but the band was white and the origins of jazz had been predominantly Black. Moreover, the name most associated with the start of jazz, Charles 'Buddy' Bolden (1877–1931), never made a record. He could have; he formed his first band in 1895, commercial recordings were being made from the very start of the twentieth century, and Bolden didn't die until fourteen years after the Original Dixieland Jass Band cut their first sides. But early record companies had little interest in jazz, and less interest in Black musicians; and anyway by 1907 Bolden was in the Louisiana State Insane Asylum, where he would spend the rest of his life.

The origins of jazz remain tantalisingly out of reach. We must rely on reports, and the reports tell us that Buddy Bolden was not only a great cornet player but a loud one. There are numerous accounts of people hearing him practise from blocks away, and of children hanging around his street to listen. One of those kids – Bolden's neighbour in multicultural New Orleans – was the Irish American clarinettist Larry Shields, who would go on to create the crowing cockerel of 'Livery Stable Blues'. But in those years when Bolden was active, from 1895 to 1907, we can't say for certain that he was playing jazz, and the term itself wasn't yet in use. We do know, however, that he played the blues, that he made use of a syncopated, ragtime style, and that he improvised – the component parts of early jazz – and the volume of Bolden's cornet was surely significant. It was something that people also noticed about Louis Armstrong's early playing, and it suggests both confidence and attitude.

High volume, indeed, is a recurrent feature of musical modernism. Beethoven's contemporaries remarked on the loudness of his symphonies; *The Rite of Spring* was loud; rock music *must* be loud, metal louder still; electronic dance music is loud; the shrieking experimental soprano of Diamanda Galás is hair-raisingly loud; noise art, from its early twentieth-century origins among the Italian futurists to the 'Japanoise' of Merzbow (Masami Akita), has been loud. In the final movement of his second piano sonata of 1948, Boulez instructed his performer to 'pulverise the sound'.

Very little modernism is polite, and along with high volume, modernist music was often jagged edged. We encounter it in the fiercely syncopated organa of Léonin, the relentless dotted rhythm of Beethoven's *Grosse Fuge* and the convulsions of Stravinsky's 'Sacrificial Dance'. And it's there in Louis Armstrong's trumpet playing from the 1920s, brash and jagged as a Picasso and crackling with life. With its stop-time choruses, wide intervals and dangerous high spirits, his trumpet lines are as vital and modern today as when he made the recordings with those other legends, Kid Ory, the Dodds brothers, Lil Hardin and Earl Hines. They must have known there was no going back, that music would not be the same again. What's more, it requires little imagination to hear in Armstrong's playing the jazz that comes next and the jazz that comes after that. We may not always recognise Armstrong's influence in Charlie Parker's music or in Ornette Coleman's, but we hear Parker and Coleman in Armstrong.

Modernism's swagger and its willingness to break things equipped it as a political tool, even if it was not always clear what its targets might be. Punk rock, for instance, though plainly rebellious, behaved like an unguided missile. But some modernists had more precise aims, however quixotic. The composer Nono, for instance, believed that the musical avant-garde might be a corollary for revolution, although his music was always too rarefied to draw the masses. In 1968, the German composer Hans Werner Henze, painting in broader strokes, attempted to unveil his cantata *The Raft of the Medusa*, dedicated to the memory of Che Guevara. Like Théodore Géricault's painting of the same name, Henze's piece told the story of the French frigate *Méduse*, which set sail for Senegal in 1816 but ran aground off the West African coast. There being only enough lifeboats for just over half the passengers and crew, the remainder were set adrift on a raft. Only fifteen of the original 146 men survived the next fortnight, some of the others having been murdered, some eaten by the survivors. *The Raft of the Medusa* is a substantial and powerful work with an element of theatre, as the chorus, starting the performance on one side of the stage (the side of the living), gradually moves, singer by singer, to the other (the side of the dead). Before the scheduled premiere in Hamburg, students, getting into the revolutionary spirit of the piece, unfurled a red flag, beneath which the choir refused to sing. Fighting broke out, the police were called, the librettist was arrested, and the evening ended with Henze himself leading the remaining members of the audience in chants of 'Ho, Ho, Ho Chi Minh'.

The American composer Julius Eastman (1940–1990) adopted a more abstract approach to political protest. Eastman belonged to a group of composers who, consciously or not, rebelled against the music of the post-war avant-garde. Because it is the opposite of the high modernism of the 1950s, minimalism is generally thought of as 'postmodernist', but if we consider it in the terms we have applied to Monteverdi and Wagner, Stravinsky and Armstrong, one has to doubt this. The early minimalism of Terry Riley, Steve Reich and Philip Glass was as radical as any serial composition, in some ways more so. Where the post-war music of Boulez, Stockhausen and Cage had been about discontinuity and moments in time, minimalist music repeated tiny rhythmic and melodic figures for minutes on end; where avant-garde music avoided tonal centres, minimalism couldn't resist them. Terry Riley's *In C* (1964) doesn't just begin and end in that key, it never leaves. If our definition of modernism is music that tears up the rule book and calls into question what music can be, then this music qualifies.

Perhaps that is what drew a radical such as Eastman into the minimalists' orbit. His music was also tonal or modal and involved much repetition and gradual change over long periods of time. But where Reich's and Glass's music of the 1970s tended to be cool and unemotional, Eastman's was not. It was more melodic than theirs and often built to quite dissonant climaxes. For all that, the political nature of the music could be missed entirely if the listener was unaware of Eastman's titles. Eastman was African American and gay, and his titles, provocative at the time and even more so today, tackled his identity head on by reclaiming the abusive language with which he had no doubt been assailed: *Nigger Faggot* (1978) was music for bell, percussion and strings; a series of pieces for four pianos called *Evil Nigger*, *Crazy Nigger* and *Gay Guerilla* (1979). During his lifetime, Eastman was best known as a singer for his 1973 recording of the extreme vocal part of Peter Maxwell Davies's

Eight Songs for a Mad King, a role he repeated with Boulez conducting members of the New York Philharmonic. But failing to find an academic outlet for his fierce intelligence, he became dependent on drugs and lived increasingly at society's margins. Following periods of homelessness, he died, unnoticed, at the age of forty-nine. It was eight months before an obituary was printed.

* * *

> Innovators always seek to revitalise, extend and reconstruct the status quo in their given fields, wherever it is needed. Quite often they are the rejects, outcasts, sub-citizens, etc. of the very societies to which they bring so much sustenance. Often they are people who endure great personal tragedy in their lives. Whatever the case, whether accepted or rejected, rich or poor, they are forever guided by that great and eternal constant – the creative urge.
>
> —John Coltrane (1926–1967),
> American composer and saxophonist

The politics of race were almost unknown in the concert hall – not that Eastman's music often made it that far – but they were a vital part of post-war jazz and various strands of pop music that began in the late 1950s and early 1960s. The free jazz movement of Ornette Coleman and Albert Ayler reclaimed jazz as Black music, 'free' being the operative word and modernity its stated aim: Coleman called his 1959 album *The Shape of Jazz to Come*. Parker, Gillespie and the beboppers had continued to use standards as the harmonic underpinning of much of their music, even if you could no longer recognise Jerome Kern's 'All the Things You Are' (rebranded 'Bird of Paradise') or Cole Porter's 'What Is This Thing Called Love?' ('Hothouse'); the free jazzers sometimes used original melodic lines, but tended to treat them heterophonously, while eschewing harmony and the chordal instruments (piano, organ, guitar) that might have provided it. When it came to the free-est of free jazz, there were plenty of people on hand to ask why it should be considered jazz at all.

One of the keys to free jazz was the quality of the noise it made. In a sense, this might be said of all jazz, for Armstrong and Gillespie's trumpets each spoke with an unmistakable voice, as did the alto and tenor saxes of Parker and Ben Webster. Miles Davis, lacking the bravura and virtuosity of either of his trumpeter forebears, instead cultivated perhaps the most distinctive instrumental voice of all, as modern as the others but shot through with the loneliness and vulnerability of Auden's 'Age of Anxiety'. Davis's sound didn't come from nowhere but was inspired, at least in part, by an actual voice.

* * *

> Somewhere in the fifties I got hooked on Miles
> Davis, especially the way he played ballads through

> his mute . . . Miles cried like a singer, and Billie [Holiday] sang like an instrumentalist, and everything they both did was wrapped in the blues.
>
> —Marvin Gaye (1939–1984), American soul singer and songwriter

Billie Holiday's singing affected everyone who heard it, her voice the antithesis of brash display, her modernism a matter of self-revelation; you didn't need to know her story of hard times and hard drugs because you heard it when she sang. Her rhythmic flexibility – just one of the things that influenced Davis – enabled her to take any song and invest it with a knowing world-weariness, while seeming to uncover deep truths the songs themselves didn't always possess. You hear the same technique at work in the singing of Frank Sinatra, Holiday's exact contemporary, who was always ready to acknowledge his debt to her. It was almost as though she was speaking to you, rather than singing for you. She brought a new dimension to jazz, and to singing in general; she also brought politics, not only when she sang her showstopper 'Strange Fruit', about the lynching of African Americans by white supremacists in 'the gallant South', but when she sang anything. The honesty of her singing can still stop you in your tracks.

* * *

> It was the music. The dirty, get-on-down music the women sang and the men played and both

> danced to, close and shameless or apart and wild . . . It made you do unwise, disorderly things. Just hearing it was like violating the law.
>
> —from *Jazz* by Toni Morrison (1931–2019), American novelist

Nina Simone said it was playing Bach that made her devote her life to music, but her dream of being a classical pianist came to nothing after she was denied entry to the Curtis Institute in Philadelphia (she believed this was because she was Black). Instead, she carried Bach into her life as a singing pianist, and you hear it in her contrapuntal playing as well as in the occasional direct quote. Her pianism was always impressive, but in the end it was hardly the point. It was Simone who recorded the second most powerful version of 'Strange Fruit', and you hear her debt to Holiday on that recording and everywhere else. It's honesty again, but Simone's voice, honey and sandpaper, was more strident than Holiday's. Like Holiday, she was best known and is best remembered for singing the songs of others, but her own songs, including 'Mississippi Goddam' and 'To Be Young, Gifted and Black' stand out. The former, an angry response to the racial violence endemic in Mississippi in the 1950s and 1960s, and to the terrorist bombing of a Baptist church in Birmingham, Alabama, that killed four girls in 1963, was intended momentarily to amuse, then shock, then horrify its audiences – which it did; the latter, a celebration, quickly became a 1970 dancefloor hit for Jamaican reggae duo Bob and Marcia, followed two years later by a gospel version from Aretha Franklin, complete with an elaborate call-and-response introduction.

By the late 1960s and early '70s, modern and modernist American music was much concerned with politics. George Crumb's electric string quartet *Black Angels* was a searing protest at the war in Vietnam (even though it didn't set out to be that), Jimi Hendrix cranked up the volume and the feedback to distort 'The Star-Spangled Banner' at the Woodstock Festival, and Marvin Gaye employed Motown Records' feel-good funk and soul to protest against racism, the war and the degradation of the natural environment on his album *What's Going On*.

* * *

> A composer cannot view the world with
> indifference. Human suffering, oppression,
> injustice . . . all that comes to me in my thoughts.
> Where there is pain, where there is injustice,
> I want to have my say through my music.
>
> —Isang Yun (1917–1995),
> Korean–German composer

In 1967 Isang Yun was living in West Germany, where he was enjoying some international renown following the premiere, the previous year, of his orchestral work *Réak*. On 17 June he and his wife were kidnapped from their Berlin apartment by the South Korean secret service and removed to Seoul, where, under torture, he confessed to spying for North Korea and was sentenced to life imprisonment. He had never been a spy; in 1963 he had visited Pyongyang, where his music had been played. The South Korean dictator Park Chung Hee was seeking to shore up his regime, and the so-called East Berlin affair – in which thirty-four European-based artists and intellectuals, including Yun, were rounded up – was part of this attempt. Following an international outcry and a petition signed by 200 of Yun's colleagues including Stravinsky, Stockhausen and the conductor Herbert von Karajan, the composer was released. He returned to West Germany in 1969 and took German citizenship.

Musicians have been persecuted throughout history, often for the causes they supported or the words they sang, more than the sound of their music. When, in the early thirteenth century, most of the troubadours of Provence were wiped out by the Albigensian Crusade, it was for their so-called 'Cathar' sympathies, not for their singing. In Chile in 1973, Victor Jara was murdered by Pinochet's military regime because of his popularity and his songs about freedom and workers. If he had sung the same tunes to words in praise of right-wing dictators, it might have been a different story. And when the Armed Islamic Group murdered Lounès Matoub in 1998 in the Kabylia region of Algeria, it wasn't his mandole playing they objected to but his role as a figurehead for Berber nationalism; of course, inspired as they were by the Taliban in Afghanistan, it is likely they hated his music too.

The Taliban and other insurgent Islamist regimes tend to object to all music, although in some cases the bans they have imposed concern the words that are being sung or the possibility that music might be accompanied by the consumption of alcohol. Still, it's hard not to believe that with all fundamentalists, religious or political, the main objections to music concern the pleasure it might bring and the perceived dangers of an unfettered imagination. The latter, in particular, is the paranoid fear of all despots. Free thinking must be checked, and when it comes to the abstraction of instrumental music, who is to say *what* is being thought?

Music can be pressed to all manner of uses, and political regimes have often pressed it to theirs. The 'Ode to Joy' from Beethoven's ninth symphony has been both the national anthem of white nationalist Rhodesia and the anthem of the European Union. In Nazi Germany, the symphony was performed annually on Hitler's birthday. In Communist China it was often wheeled out for special occasions. Beethoven's music in general occupied a special place in China, both before and after the revolution of 1949, and again after the Cultural Revolution. The attraction, in part, was the legend of the man and his endurance against the odds, but also the nature of the music and the way much of it embodies that quality of perseverance. Where the *Appassionata* sonata had made Lenin feel an empathy he worried was weakness, for many Chinese people, Beethoven's music, especially the third, fifth and ninth symphonies, encouraged revolutionary zeal.

In the 1930s, the Nazis turned not only to Beethoven, but to Wagner and other German composers of the past to bolster their delusion of Aryan supremacy. It helped that Wagner,

Hitler's favourite composer, had himself been virulently antisemitic. We can't know what Wagner would have thought of Nazism (he was dead before Hitler was born), but the association of the composer with the Third Reich remains strong enough that his music is still unwelcome in Israel. We do know what Carl Orff (1895–1982) thought of the Nazis; he saw them as a way to get ahead and developed his teaching system, known as Schulwerk, with the Hitler Youth in mind. They turned him down, but amid the junking of much modernist music and the murder of Jewish composers, *Carmina Burana* remained a Nazi favourite.

In the Soviet Union, modernism had at first been encouraged after the revolution. The notion of total revolution included the arts and the experimentation of composers such as Nikolai Roslavets, Arthur Lourié and Alexander Mosolov was supported, particularly if their pieces had titles such as *The Iron Foundry*, Mosolov's three minutes of mechanistic brutality composed in 1927. But artistic freedom did not last long. Perhaps the Soviet authorities realised that, minus its title, *The Iron Foundry* might be about almost anything: a battle, say, or a sacrificial virgin dancing herself to death in pagan Russia. Music without words became a matter of suspicion, decried as 'formalist' – art for art's sake – and not the best use of a Soviet composer's time. It didn't save them from occasional condemnation, but star composers Sergei Prokofiev and Dimitri Shostakovich were permitted to go on writing symphonies and concertos and string quartets so long as they also produced cantatas with titles such as *On*

Guard for Peace (Prokofiev) and *The Sun Shines Over Our Motherland* (Shostakovich). Others, such as Galina Ustvolskaya, kept their heads down. Ustvolskaya was an uncompromisingly original composer whose music was bound up with her fierce spirituality and whose pieces involved extremes of dissonance and dynamic (abruptly switching from *pppppp* to *ffffff*) along with passages of relentless repetition.

One of the stranger official attitudes to music during the Cold War period was the clandestine sponsorship by the US State Department and the CIA of modernist composers such as Elliott Carter, whose thorny first string quartet of 1951 seems to have been a particular favourite with the spooks (so clandestine was the support that Carter himself was unaware of it until decades later). The idea was to demonstrate that the West was progressive and open, in contrast to the Soviet Union, where writing modernist music might land you in a gulag, and so festivals of modernist music were staged in Europe with discreetly laundered CIA money. No doubt oblivious to the paradox, the CIA also funded the animated film of *Animal Farm*, George Orwell's novel that, among other things, is an indictment of propaganda.

During the Second World War, big-band swing had been more openly promoted in a similarly ideological way. Jazz had been the invention of African Americans, Benny Goodman and Artie Shaw were Jews, and the standards of jazz were the work of songwriters whose original names had been Israel Beilin (Irving Berlin), Jacob Gershwine (George Gershwin) and Hyman Arluck (Harold Arlen). The United States might have been segregated, antisemitism rife, but jazz was still a way to assert anti-Nazi sentiments. The Nazis themselves never banned jazz outright – it was too popular – but they placed comical restrictions on the music that included upper limits on syncopation (10 per cent) and swing (20 per cent) in any jazz composition, and the outlawing of scat and plucked bass. The rules around tempo were especially hazy: too slow and the music was deemed to be 'Jewishly gloomy'; too fast and it risked 'negroid excess'.

* * *

> I had another dream the other day about music critics. They were small and rodent-like with padlocked ears, as if they had stepped out of a painting by Goya.
>
> —Igor Stravinsky

According to Stravinsky, the most valid form of criticism was a new piece of music, and modernist music has always given rise to *that* sort of criticism. After serialism came post-serialism; after bebop, post-bop; after punk, post-punk; and, in all the arts, postmodernism was the defining ism of the late twentieth and early twenty-first centuries. The terms are largely meaningless, but much of the music is as worth our time as what went before.

Most postmodernist art, while a riposte to modernism, was also made possible by it. So much modernist music –

especially that of the mid-twentieth century – involved a kind of creative cul-de-sac from which there was only one way out. For instance, one- and two-chord punk rock produced the wave of post-punk singer–songwriters that followed (Elvis Costello, say, or Rickie Lee Jones), who owed much to punk's music and its attitudes (which in punk's case were the same things).

Bebop might have led to free jazz, but before that it had spawned its opposite in the so-called 'Birth of the Cool' sessions of 1949, in which Miles Davis and Gerry Mulligan, who could play bop with the best, lowered the music's temperature and its pace. The fractured melody of bebop remained but, at the slower tempo, it was easier for listeners to put the pieces together. Davis's *Kind of Blue* (1959) with Bill Evans, arguably the culmination of what had begun ten years earlier, was a masterpiece in anyone's book and almost made modern jazz mainstream.

Pierre Boulez once referred to a post-war 'zero hour' that involved the systematisation of all aspects of musical composition, Schoenberg's twelve-tone rows applied to durations, dynamics and music's other parameters; utter systematisation. But a 'zero hour', by definition, is not the future, and Boulez's single piece of total or 'integral' surrealism – *Structures 1a* for two pianos (1950) – lasted approximately three and a half minutes, after which he felt no need for such restrictions.

Since Boulez and Cage were in touch at the time, it would be fair to regard Cage's *4'33"*, composed two years later and surely the ultimate 'zero hour', as a riposte to integral serialism, the calculation and systematisation of the latter replaced by a silent piano and the ambient sounds of a concert hall, its audience waiting for something to happen. But wasn't *4'33"* modernist too? What about La Monte Young's *Piano Piece #1 for Terry Riley* (1960)? The pianist is instructed to place the flat side of a grand piano against a wall and push; if the piano goes through the wall, the player should keep pushing regardless of further obstacles, the piece being over when exhaustion sets in. Or Annea Lockwood's 'piano burning' from *Piano Transplants* (1968)? Modernist? Here is the score of that piece.

> *Set upright piano (not a grand) in an open space*
> *with the lid closed.*
> *Spill a little lighter fluid on a twist of paper and*
> *place inside, near the pedals.*
> *Light it.*
> *Balloons may be stapled to the piano.*
> *Play whatever pleases you for as long as you can.*

The year of its first performance was a time of 'happenings' – public arts events, often of an iconoclastic if unclassifiable nature – and Lockwood's 'piano burning' certainly fits the description. But perhaps the undeniable theatricality of the 'piece' creates a link all the way back to the dramatic works of Monteverdi. In Lockwood's 'piano burning' the action and the music are as inseparable as they had been in *L'Orfeo*, and the New Zealander did intend her piece to be sound as much as spectacle. But were the plinks and plonks of snapping piano wires a critique of modernist music or, perhaps, modernism's next phase?

Annea Lockwood at a piano burning

Lockwood described how stagings of 'piano burning' tended to begin in a carnival atmosphere but would invariably end with the audience falling quiet to listen to the gentle crackles of the fire, as though in mourning for the instrument. This might be thought of as a common response to modernist music and modernist art in general: excitement for the new, tempered with nostalgia for what is lost.

5

RECORDING MUSIC: FROM 1900 TO THE PRESENT

ON THE EVENING OF 19 MAY 1924, the famous English cellist Beatrice Harrison played a duet with a nightingale in her Surrey garden. Miss Harrison, who a few years earlier had made the first recording of Elgar's cello concerto, liked to practise outdoors and had often found herself duetting with the bird. Somehow she had persuaded the BBC that they should come to Oxted, south of London, to broadcast the event. At the appointed hour, she began to play her cello, but the bird stayed silent. On she played regardless, the imagined duo just a solo, until, in the nick of time, the nightingale found his voice. It is a famous moment in early broadcasting, one the BBC was forced to repeat for several years. But in 2022 it was revealed that the 'nightingale' in the original broadcast had probably been a bird impersonator, a *siffleur* who performed on stage as Madame Saberon. The BBC had had her on standby in case the bird got cold feet. Where microphones are involved, there will often be trickery.

When Elvis Presley recorded 'Heartbreak Hotel' in his first session for RCA Victor in 1956, the producer felt the singer's voice would benefit from a hollow acoustic – he was, after all, meant to be 'down at the end of Lonely Street'. So Presley was dispatched to the far end of the studio, some distance from the microphone, and told to sing up. In 1974, when Herbert von Karajan and the Berlin Philharmonic recorded Schoenberg's Variations for Orchestra, an ever-shifting kaleidoscope

Edward Elgar making an acoustic recording with London Symphony Orchestra in 1914

of complex orchestral colour, the conductor and his Deutsche Grammophon engineers reseated the players between variations to achieve the ideal balance and clarity among the instruments. Two years later in Toronto, Glenn Gould recorded a selection of Sibelius's piano music with microphones set up at various distances from his instrument so that, in the final mix, it was possible to move the listener's ears closer to the piano, then farther away, then very close, then very distant; acoustic orchestration, Gould's producer called it.

And why not? A recording is not a live performance, even if there will always be purists who feel everything should be done in a single, unedited take. Of course you can do that too, just as a feature film could be a play filmed from a single angle, but when there is so much more you can bring to the experience, why would you? The controlled acoustics of sound recording enabled us to hear musical details we might not hear in a live performance, and this altered the way we listened to music and understood it. It changed the kinds of music we could hear and, in some cases, the nature of music itself.

Technology has been part of music since it first occurred to someone that the stone tool they were using might *sound* better if slightly modified. Instruments have been invented, then improved, and with technological advance came musical change. The invention of the saxophone by the Belgian Adolphe Sax in the early 1840s almost immediately altered the sound of military bands; the electric guitar, invented in 1932, originally allowed the guitar to be heard in the context of big band jazz, but was very soon taken up by gospel singers, most notably Sister Rosetta Tharpe, whose expertise and originality (and not a few of her actual licks) were widely copied until the instrument became the mainstay of 1950s rock and roll. But nothing changed music more than the invention of sound recording, at first acoustic, then electric, then digital.

Acoustic recording involved singing or playing into a large horn that sent the sounds to a membrane, the vibrations from which agitated a stylus that cut into a wax cylinder or disc. Electric recording, which began in the early 1920s, came courtesy of the invention of the microphone.

The microphone itself, it might be argued, became the single most influential instrument of the twentieth century, not only for its ability to pick up sounds and transmit them to a disc or later to tape, but because it allowed popular singers to sing intimately. Before the microphone, singers had to belt in order to be heard over a band. The microphone was the difference between Ethel Merman and Frank Sinatra.

We now take it for granted, but it is worth considering what the experience of music was like prior to recording. If you lived at the beginning of the twentieth century, you would have been lucky to hear each of Beethoven's nine symphonies once in your life. You would have heard them live, which would have required access to an orchestra, so you'd have to have lived in a Western city. The alternative would have been one of those piano-duet reductions, a good way to get to know the notes of the symphonies, but not their orchestral sound. Radio, which came along in the 1920s, could bring an orchestra into your home; classical music stations meant you could hear Beethoven's symphonies quite frequently; twenty-four-hour classical stations would let you hear them by accident; and commercial recordings – in ever-higher fidelity – allowed you, if you were interested, to compare different interpretations of the symphonies. By the start of the twenty-first century, there were hundreds of recordings of the fifth symphony alone, and online some of them could be heard for free.

That's rapid change: from piano reductions to wax cylinders to shellac and vinyl, to cassette tapes and compact discs, iPods and streaming services, all in a little over a century. It enabled two extreme modes of listening, the first an intense encounter with the music, akin to study; the second, background music which barely involved listening at all.

Recordings collapsed both history and geography. In a Western concert hall at the start of the twentieth century you would have heard highlights of 150 years of Western art music (a generous estimate); additionally, music halls and theatres would have given you current popular songs, and domestic pianos the means of singing them at home. But the idea that you could be anywhere in the world and, at the flick of a switch, listen to 900 years of music was unthinkable, and so was having ready access to music of all cultures. In the twentieth century, thanks to sound recording, Japanese people became familiar with jazz, Swedes discovered the blues and Finns found the tango; via the Beatles, everyone heard the Indian sitar. West African musicians heard rock music (full as it was of West African roots), stripped it down, built it back up and sold it to Europeans and Americans in the form of albums by Salif Keita and Youssou N'Dour.

One of the first uses to which sound recording was put was the capturing of traditional music, much of which was considered endangered, on phonographs that etched sound into wax cylinders or discs called 'records'. Across Europe, collectors travelled on sometimes arduous journeys to meet people in rural areas where they would try to persuade them to sing. It wasn't an easy job, as the composer and collector Percy Grainger found when he attempted to collect the song 'Dublin Bay' from an elderly man in a Lincolnshire workhouse, but returning with a phonograph made it easier.

'In 1905, when I first met its singer – Mr Deane of Hibbaldstowe – he was in the workhouse at Brigg,' Grainger recalled. 'I started to note down his "Dublin Bay", but the workhouse matron asked me to stop, as Mr Deane's heart was very weak and the singing of the old song – which he had not sung for forty years – brought back poignant memories to him and made him burst into tears. I reluctantly desisted. But a year or so later, when I had acquired a phonograph, I returned to get Mr Deane's tune . . . I thought he might as well die singing it as die without singing it.

'I found him in the hospital ward of the workhouse, with a great gash in his head . . . having fallen down stairs. He was very proud of his wound, and insisted that he was far too weak to sing. "All right, Mr. Deane," I said to him, "you needn't sing yourself; but I would like you to hear some records made by other singers in these parts." He had not heard half a record through before he said, impulsively: "I'll sing for you, yoong mahn."'

* * *

> All the songs I've heard in my life was folk songs.
> I never heard horses sing one of them yet.
>
> —Big Bill Broonzy (1903–1958), American blues singer and guitarist

Traditional songs and dance tunes were preserved in a range of manners, from the creative to the academic to the commercial. Grainger not only recorded songs, he also arranged them, sometimes extravagantly, often preserving the melodic ornamentation the original singer had employed while adding dense, chromatic harmonies to squeeze every ounce of emotion from the song; Bartók, as mentioned, drew the raw sound of folk music into his orchestral and chamber works. In the United States, Frances Densmore made it her life's work to record Native American songs across much of the North American continent and write about them, and later folklorists, such as Alan Lomax, did the same for the blues. Blues recordings were sold as 'race records', the term implying that only African Americans would be interested in listening to them, and they sold in large numbers. Blues is one of the world's youngest forms of traditional music and one of the last, because in a world where everything is recorded there is no need – or possibility – of purely oral transmission. We're told that blues sprang up among rural Black communities in the Mississippi Delta around the end of the nineteenth century or the beginning of the twentieth, but we can't pinpoint the moment or the people responsible for it. In old age, L.V. Thomas (who in 1930, going by the name of 'Elvie' Thomas, recorded with Geeshie Wiley) stated that in 1902, when she first took up the guitar, there was blues 'even back then'. As Greil Marcus has remarked, this implies that Thomas recalled a time *before* there was blues, which would suggest that the music began in the 1890s, a few years before jazz, to which it bequeathed its harmonic templates. What we can say with certainty is that blues draws on earlier African American musical traditions, the spiritual and the field holler, their call-and-response forms reflected in the repeated lines of blues.

Although jazz came out of blues, the first blues recording postdates the sides cut in 1917 by the Original Dixieland Jass Band. Sheet music of blues songs composed by professional songwriters such as W.C. Handy was being published from 1914, but sound recording didn't begin until the early 1920s. This was blues as a form of novelty entertainment featuring a vaudeville singer with a band, and the success of Mamie Smith's 'Crazy Blues', which sold 75,000 copies in its first month, showed there was a market for it. Ma Rainey and Bessie Smith, who both made their first records in 1923, were still essentially vaudevillians but brought elements of something rawer, something more authentic. Even so, many of these early blues recordings are hard to distinguish from early jazz records, and often share the same personnel. The famous 1925 recording of Bessie Smith singing Handy's 'Saint Louis Blues' features Louis Armstrong on cornet.

But then came Blind Lemon Jefferson – a singer and his guitar. At first he recorded gospel songs under a pseudonym, but by mid-1926 he was making records such as 'Long Lonesome Blues', the sales of which hit six figures. This was the real thing, Blind Lemon moaning and wailing, stretching and bending notes, pulling and sliding on the strings of his guitar, the voice and the instrument a single organism.

Over more than a century, blues scarcely changed. Following the Great Migration of African Americans from the rural south of the United States to the industrialised north, the electric blues that emanated from Chicago was louder and punchier, and later, as the basis of heavy rock, the music acquired a hitherto unanticipated grandiloquence. But those eight-, twelve- and sixteen-bar templates that gave early blues its structures remained; if you took them away, it was no longer blues.

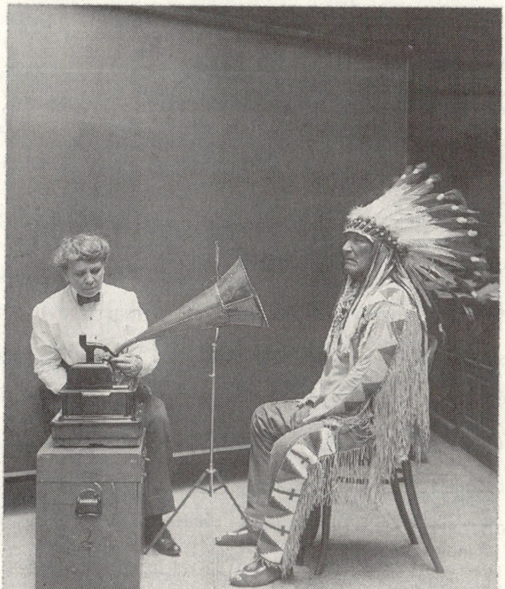

Frances Densmore recording Mountain Chief in 1916

In the 1950s and '60s, something else extraordinary happened to blues, and it was because of sound recording. The records of Muddy Waters, Howlin' Wolf, Little Walter and a host of other urban blues musicians rekindled interest in a music that had almost died during the Second World War. Among its fans were British 'rhythm and blues' bands like the Rolling Stones and the Animals. In response to a growing interest in the origins of the music, folklorists, festival promoters and record producers went in search of the original country blues artists. These were men and women who had performed as young people but given it up as the popularity of the music had waned. Now, in old age, they brushed up their guitar playing and went out on the festival circuit and into the recording studio.

Son House, who was born in Mississippi in 1902, cut some poorly selling discs in 1930, then drove a tractor and later worked as a porter for the New York Central Railroad. In 1964, he was discovered at a railway station in upstate New York, oblivious to the fact of the blues revival. The following year, he recorded a number of tracks, including a searing account of 'Death Letter', a version of a song called 'My Black Mama' that he'd first recorded thirty-five years earlier. There can be few blues recordings more powerful than 'Death Letter', House's voice strong and cracked as he almost attacks his slide guitar.

Elizabeth Cotten's story was more remarkable yet. Born in 1893 in North Carolina, she worked casually as a domestic servant from the age of nine, joining her mother in full-time service at twelve. She taught herself guitar, which she played

Piedmont style, but left-handed and without restringing the instrument, so her index finger picked the bass line and her thumb the melody. She also wrote songs, one of which was called 'Freight Train'. But when she was only in her mid-teens, a deacon of her church told her she must stop singing and playing, and for half a century she did, except occasionally in church itself. In the 1940s she moved to Washington, DC, where she worked as a housekeeper and seasonally in a department store. This was where she helped a lost little girl called Peggy find her grateful mother. The mother was the composer Ruth Crawford Seeger, and Cotten went to work as the family's housekeeper and cook. Peggy's father was the folklorist Charles Seeger, and her older stepbrother was Pete Seeger, the folk singer and banjo player. Cotten worked for the Seegers for some years before Peggy one day discovered her playing Peggy's guitar.

Elizabeth Cotten playing her guitar upside down

In 1957, Peggy, by now a folk singer herself, sang Cotten's 'Freight Train' while touring Europe, and a performance in England was recorded. Now the song took on a life of its own. This was during the British skiffle craze, when up-tempo versions of American blues and country songs were very popular, and in short order Chas McDevitt and Nancy Whiskey recorded 'Freight Train' (without crediting Cotten) and made it a hit. Other recordings followed in the United Kingdom and the United States. The Quarrymen, later the Beatles, included the song in their sets from 1957, with John Lennon on lead vocals. In the end, Cotten received her writing credit and royalties – the Seegers saw to that – and in 1958 she recorded her own version for Peggy's brother Mike, released on the Folkways label with thirteen other tracks as *Folksongs and Instrumentals with Guitar*. She was sixty-five years old and went on performing into her nineties.

That so many famous blues recordings were of relatively elderly singers and guitarists underlines the fact that this was a traditional form of music, a *remembered* music. Like most of the performers, the blues itself had lain dormant through the middle of the twentieth century. The opposite was true of jazz, which was recorded more or less from the start. Duke Ellington was among the first to understand that sound recording could do more than sell records and make jazz popular; it could also expand the music's capabilities. In 1935, the Ellington Orchestra recorded 'Reminiscing in Tempo', thirteen minutes of music spread across four 10-inch 78-rpm sides, to each of which the Columbia record company attached the label 'foxtrot'. It was hardly that!

'Reminiscing in Tempo' had its critics. The producer John Hammond wrote a review in *DownBeat* magazine entitled 'The Tragedy of Duke Ellington' in which he lambasted the composer for the vapidity of this new music, comparing it unfavourably to Debussy and Delius, and arguing that in composing such 'formless and shallow' stuff (intended by Ellington as a tribute to his late mother), the African American Ellington had shut 'his eyes to the abuses being heaped upon his race'. Hammond was white.

What was happening, of course, was that Ellington was being original and modernist. Jazz had been changing its shape and form from the start, and Ellington recognised that it did not have to be restricted by the length of a three-minute side. 'Reminiscing in Tempo' was just the beginning of an exploration of the potential of jazz, which, alongside a stream of Ellington's swing hits, included large-scale works such as the symphony *Black, Brown and Beige* (1941) and, from the mid-1960s, his three Sacred Concerts – really jazz liturgies, though Ellington always denied that. What could hardly be denied was that jazz was becoming sophisticated. With *Black, Brown and Beige*, Ellington inaugurated his annual seasons at Carnegie Hall; the first Sacred Concert had its premiere in San Francisco's Grace Cathedral, the second was written for the Cathedral of St John the Divine in New York, and the third for Westminster Abbey. This was forty-five years after Louis Armstrong had recorded 'Potato Head Blues'.

In 1971, two years before Ellington's third Sacred Concert,

Carla Bley released her triple album *Escalator Over the Hill*, a jazz opera with words by Paul Haines. Unlike Ellington's extended works, it was a studio project from start to finish, three years in the making and unrealisable in concert or on the opera stage. Bley brought together musicians of varying stripes such as free jazz stalwarts Don Cherry and Gato Barbieri, the versatile bebop singer Sheila Jordan, English blues singer Paul Jones, Jack Bruce, the bass player of rock trio Cream, and a young Linda Ronstadt. Stylistically, as might be expected, the work was eclectic. Bley's typically brassy sound – two parts Kurt Weill to one part Salvation Army band – was embellished with everything from free-jazz noise to bluegrass breaks, extended and distorted with studio effects. Going back to 'Potato Head Blues' as a point of reference, it is hard to see a through line to Bley's *Escalator*. Jazz had shot off in so many directions, and nearly all of them were on this triple album.

Similar techniques were at play in pop music. The Beach Boys' *Pet Sounds* and the Beatles' *Revolver* and *Sgt Pepper's Lonely Hearts Club Band* were, likewise, studio creations. Working in this way involved creative collaboration with engineers and producers and it took time. The Beatles' first album, *Please Please Me* (1963), had been recorded in less than ten hours; four years later, *Sgt Pepper* took 129 days. And there was another correspondence between modern jazz and pop. Both forms of music had started out as dance music; now they weren't. It is often overlooked amid its other innovations, but *Sgt Pepper* was the first pop album to print the lyrics to its songs. This was music for sitting down and listening to.

In some ways it was Miles Davis's move into electronic music that ushered in the biggest change in jazz. It wasn't just that *In a Silent Way* (1969) drew on the sounds of rock music, or that *Bitches Brew* (1970) embraced the gestures and rhythms of rock – jazz had always been a sponge for other styles. It was the way these albums were made that was so radical. By the end of the 1960s, jazz had begun to lose touch with the blues (in some quarters, at least), but the one thing that had remained constant was improvisation. The details of jazz were made up on the spot, even if recording the music froze that spontaneity. On Davis's *Kind of Blue*, which is perhaps familiar to more people than any other jazz album, the players never rehearsed; they were handed a few scales on scraps of paper, then winged it.

Davis's new albums started out the same way, but this time there were no final takes. When the musicians left the studio after the sessions, the producer Teo Macero got to work making the albums from the raw material they had recorded. Using tape loops, delay and overdubbing, but above all close editing, Macero was doing a lot more than post-production; he was, in effect, composing the final music. *In a Silent Way* and *Bitches Brew* featured some of the most famous jazz musicians of their day – in addition to Davis, figures such as saxophonist Wayne Shorter, keyboard players Chick Corea, Herbie Hancock and Joe Zawinul, drummers Tony Williams, Jack DeJohnette and Billy Cobham, bassist Dave Holland and guitarist John McLaughlin – but their contributions amounted to the raw material for Macero's work. The structure of the music was his.

Many of Macero's techniques were similar to those used to make the pop music of the day – *Sgt Pepper* had employed overdubs and tape loops – but the real inspiration for his work was *musique concrète*, the term given to compositions created by editing pre-recorded sounds. These sounds, although of intrinsic interest, were not necessarily 'musical' – sometimes they were industrial in origin; the music resulted from the way they were assembled in a technique rather like the making of a collage.

The earliest example of *musique concrète* is generally considered to be *Ta'abir al-Zār* (The Expression of Zār), made by the Egyptian composer Halim El-Dabh in 1944 when he took a wire recorder onto the streets of Cairo, disguised in full niqab, and attended a zār ceremony – a public exorcism practised by women in the Middle East and the Horn of Africa ('zār' is the Arabic word for demon). Editing his recording and adding reverberation, El-Dabh created an intense and rather hypnotic work of a little over twenty minutes.

By 1948, Paris had become the centre of activity for tape music in the Studio d'Essai, founded by Pierre Schaeffer, who coined the term *musique concrète*. One of his students, Éliane Radigue (b. 1932), is a particularly interesting figure in that having been trained in *musique concrète*, she was drawn to create tape music that used only electronic sound, her work gaining a kind of purity from the avoidance of non-electronic source material. Using microphone and tape feedback, and later synthesisers, she created long, drone-like pieces in which tones and textures changed very slowly. The patient listener feels these changes as part of a meditative experience, and it is not surprising that Radigue's major three-hour work, her *Trilogie de la mort* (Trilogy of Death), should be based on *The Tibetan Book of the Dead*.

In her seventies Radigue suddenly abandoned electronic composition, devoting herself to writing for instruments, but the music hardly changed. The pieces were still immensely slow and the shifting of pitch gradual and microtonal. If there was now an extra element of humanity in the music, there was still the same concern with the quality of sound that had characterised her earlier work.

Eliane Radigue in her studio

From the start, sound quality was an obsession of those who recorded music, but the swift progress from wax cylinder to laptop brought more than higher fidelity. Sound technology, which had begun as a means of preserving performance and conveying it to listeners, then created an industry for the exploitation of music in our lives, had, by the twenty-first century, become the medium for cheaply recording, editing, mixing, mastering and disseminating music. It could all be achieved on the same device, and often enough this device was how the finished product was received and played back.

Had something been lost? Of course. Was something gained? Undoubtedly. But the laptop or smartphone did not replace the rock bands or jazz trios, choirs or orchestras, and as Éliane Radigue's career demonstrated, technology could sometimes be replaced by human beings. The fundamentals of music still applied.

EPILOGUE: WHAT IS MUSIC?

> A single strum of the strings or even one pluck is too complex, too complete in itself to admit any theory. Between this complex sound – so strong that it can stand alone – and that point of intense silence preceding it, called ma, there is a metaphysical continuity that defies analysis.
>
> —Tōru Takemitsu (1930–1996), Japanese composer

IT WILL NOT HAVE GONE UNNOTICED that up to now this book has avoided defining the term 'music'. The most accurate definition is probably John Cage's. He said music was 'organised sound', which covers all bases, since it leaves room for the listener to do the organising. But Cage's definition doesn't get to the heart of music's importance, and doesn't attempt to. The trouble is that this universal importance is itself hard to pin down (we're back to music's *not* being a universal language), because different cultures and individual people within those cultures find music important for a range of reasons. But is there some aspect of the musical experience that is common to us all? Is there a *need* for music – even

Takemitsu's single strum or pluck – that is universal? The most avowedly unmusical among us, left alone in a room with a drum or a piano, a guitar or a child's glockenspiel, will be unable, in time, to resist coaxing a sound from it. Is this the need? Are we simply and wordlessly verifying our existence as we tap at the drum? Is this the significance of music Steven Pinker can't explain?

* * *

> Behold her, single in the field,
> Yon solitary Highland Lass!
> Reaping and singing by herself;
> Stop here, or gently pass!
>
> —from 'The Solitary Reaper' by
> William Wordsworth (1770–1850), English poet

Someone working alone in a field is today more likely to have earbuds in than to be singing for themselves, but singing, even solitary singing, is unlikely to vanish from the earth.

In Siegfried Sassoon's poem 'Everyone Sang', written in 1919, the act of singing becomes a metaphor for freedom, and it is specifically group singing, the spontaneous choir of the title, that the poem celebrates. It was not only in the nineteenth century that choral societies could be political. In the years leading to the re-establishment of Estonia's independence from the Soviet Union in 1991, choral singing was the preferred form of nonviolent protest and the national song festival its focal point; this was the so-called 'Singing Revolution'. The songs sung by the Estonians had appropriately patriotic words, but the mere fact of choral singing can be deemed political: we are united; we cooperate with others, losing ourselves in the crowd; the effect, as Sassoon put it, is to be 'filled with such delight / As prisoned birds must find in freedom'.

Wordsworth's poem 'The Solitary Reaper' was not written from firsthand experience, but in response to his friend Thomas Wilkinson's manuscript *Tours to the British Mountains* (published in 1824), in which the author recalled something he had seen and heard on a journey through the Scottish Highlands.

'Passed a Female who was reaping alone,' Wilkinson wrote. 'She sung in Erse as she bended over her sickle; the sweetest human voice I ever heard: her strains were tenderly melancholy, and felt delicious, long after they were heard no more.' The 'voice so thrilling' that Wilkinson heard, and that Wordsworth turned into poetry, had nothing to do with the words the reaper sang because they were in 'Erse' (the old name for Gaelic), which neither man would have understood. It was her voice alone that was so beguiling. Similarly, for Sassoon's singers, who have no words in any language, it is the sudden outburst of song that provokes the delight and sense of freedom, and an almost spiritual union described in the final lines: 'O, but Everyone / Was a bird; and the song was wordless; the singing will never be done.'

It will never be done because the impulse to sing is

fundamental. Many of us sing in public – in a choir, at a football match, at church, in a karaoke bar – but most of us sing in private, or we may whistle or hum. We do it at home, under our breath, perhaps, or in the shower when we think no one is listening; often it is unbidden. And in our domesticity we may also improvise as a form of communication – perhaps connection is a better word – with a baby.

Recording songs of the Chippewa (Ojibwe) and Menominee tribes in Minnesota and Wisconsin, early in the twentieth century, Frances Densmore found that lullabies were not 'composed' or 'received in dreams', which is how 'important songs' came, but 'developed gradually from the gentle crooning sounds with which the mothers soothed the little children' – a composition from an improvised beginning. And yet, when she requested a lullaby, sometimes the women sang 'only a sort of "endless tune"'.

This is surely close to the source of all music. It is from domestic beginnings that music burgeons and to which it returns, again and again.

* * *

Listen to this song, this singer . . .
I sing the ruins into money;
I sing the pebbles into pennies;
I sing the mountains into butter tubs;
I sing the stones into eggs.

—from the *Kanteletar,* trad. Finnish

On 30 April 2023 at the Canberra International Music Festival, Kalkadunga man William Barton walked slowly through the audience, singing his song 'Kalkadunga Yurdu', as the Brodsky Quartet waited for him on stage playing a supporting drone. Barton then took up his didgeridoo and, together with the quartet, performed his extended composition *Square Circles Beneath the Red Desert Sand*. Since the boy who searched for a tree with his father turned into the world's most famous didgeridoo player, Barton's singing has become more and more important to his performances, and 'Kalkadunga Yurdu', which he composed in his early teens, is his signature song; he sang it for his father as his father took his last breaths. The song is not fixed – its details are always changing – but it is recognisably the same each time he sings it, and Barton has sung it for the likes of Herbie Hancock, Yo-Yo Ma and members of the Berlin Philharmonic, with Icehouse's Iva Davies and Basement Jaxx. *Kalkadungu*, the large-scale piece he composed with Matthew Hindson, has been performed (with Barton as soloist) by orchestras in Australia, North America and Europe, at venues including New York's Carnegie Hall and the Mariinsky Theatre in St Petersburg.

Barton's fame as a virtuoso of his instrument and increasingly as a composer shouldn't obscure the significance of the song he has carried with him since childhood. Like Elizabeth Cotten's 'Freight Train', also the work of a child, it comes from a precise place (Mount Isa, Queensland in Barton's case; Chapel Hill, North Carolina in Cotten's) and from a moment in time. Barton and Cotten must have thought their songs worth keeping, but neither could have guessed their greater significance in the future.

Hildegard's nuns praising God in their Rhineland abbey; Haydn entertaining his prince in a castle on a reclaimed swamp in Hungary; the young Halim El-Dabh thinking it was a good idea to borrow a wire recorder from Middle East Radio and take it onto the Cairo streets; the Sugarhill Gang releasing 'Rapper's Delight': you never know how far your music – your 'organised sound' – will go or for how long, or who it will reach. You also don't know what your sound might mean to those who hear it next week or next year or next century and, in their own minds – their own imaginations – make it theirs.

* * *

> . . . you are the music while the music lasts.
>
> —from *Four Quartets* by
> T.S. Eliot (1888–1965), American poet

Further Reading

Abdurraqib, Hanif. *A Little Devil in America: In Praise of Black Performance*. New York: Random House, 2021.

Atherton, Michael. *A Coveted Possession: The Rise and Fall of the Piano in Australia*. Carlton, Vic: Black Inc., 2018.

Bailey, Philip. *Yehudiana: Reliving the Menuhin Odyssey*. Robertson, NSW: Fountaindale Press, 2010.

Bebey, Francis. *African Music: A People's Art*. Brooklyn, NY: Hill, 1975.

Bellaigue, Christopher de. *The Islamic Enlightenment: The Modern Struggle Between Faith and Reason*. London: Bodley Head, 2017.

Booth, Mark W. *The Experience of Songs*. New Haven, CT: Yale University Press, 1981.

Braudel, Fernand. *A History of Civilizations*. New York: Allen Lane, 1993.

Brendel, Franz. *Geschichte der Musik in Italien, Deutschland und Frankreich: von den ersten christlichen Zeiten bis auf die Gegenwart; 22 Vorlesungen gehalten zu Leipzig im Jahre 1850*. Leipzig: Bruno Hinze, 1852.

Burlingame, Jon. *Music for Prime Time: A History of American Television Themes and Scoring*. New York: Oxford University Press, 2023.

Burkholder, James Peter, Donald Jay Grout and Claude V. Palisca. *A History of Western Music*. New York: Norton, 2019.

Cai, Jindong and Sheila Melvin. *Beethoven in China: How the Great Composer Became an Icon in the People's Republic*. Melbourne: Penguin, 2015.

Campbell, Edward and Peter O'Hagan. *The Cambridge Stravinsky Encyclopedia*. Cambridge: Cambridge University Press, 2021.

Carroll, Mark. *Music and Ideology in Cold War Europe*. Cambridge: Cambridge University Press, 2003.

Celenza, Anna Harwell. *Jazz Italian Style: From Its Origins in New Orleans to Fascist Italy and Sinatra*. Cambridge: Cambridge University Press, 2017.

Chaudhuri, Amit. *Finding the Raga: An Improvisation on Indian Music*. London: Faber, 2021.

Cole, Ross. *The Folk: Music, Modernity and the Political Imagination*. Oakland: University of California Press, 2021.

Coleman, Nick. *Voices: How a Great Singer Can Change Your Life*. London: Penguin, 2018.

Craske, Oliver. *Indian Sun: The Life and Music of Ravi Shankar*. London: Faber, 2020.

Davidson, Caroline. *The Captain's Apprentice: Ralph Vaughan Williams and the Story of a Folk Song*. London: Chatto & Windus, 2022.

Densmore, Frances. *The American Indians and Their Music*. New York: The Womans Press, 1926.

Dubois, Laurent. *The Banjo: America's African Instrument*. Cambridge, MA: Belknap Press, 2016.

Eisenberg, Evan. *The Recording Angel: Music, Records and Culture from Aristotle to Zappa*. New York: McGraw-Hill, 1987.

Finnegan, Ruth, ed. *The Penguin Book of Oral Poetry*. London: Allen Lane, 1978.

Fisk, Josiah, ed. *Composers on Music: Eight Centuries of Writing*, 2nd edition. Boston: Northwestern University Press, 1997.

Ford, Andrew. *Composer to Composer: Conversations about Contemporary Music*. St Leonards, NSW: Allen & Unwin, 1993.

Ford, Andrew. *Earth Dances: Music in Search of the Primitive*. Carlton, Vic: Black Inc., 2015.

Ford, Andrew. *Illegal Harmonies: Music in the Modern Age*, 3rd edition. Collingwood, Vic: Black Inc., 2011.

Ford, Andrew and Anni Heino. *The Song Remains the Same: 800 Years of Love Songs, Laments and Lullabies*. Carlton, Vic: La Trobe University Press, 2019.

Gay'wu Group of Women. *Songspirals: Sharing Women's Wisdom of Country Through Songlines*. Sydney: Allen & Unwin, 2019.

Giddins, Gary. *Visions of Jazz: The First Century*. New York: Oxford University Press, 1998.

Gottlieb, Robert, ed. *Reading Jazz: A Gathering of Autobiography, Reportage and Criticism from 1919 to Now*. New York: Bloomsbury, 1997.

Gould, Elaine. *Behind Bars: The Definitive Guide to Music Notation*. London: Faber Music, 2011.

Graeber, David and David Wengrow. *The Dawn of Everything: A New History of Humanity*. London: Allen Lane, 2021.

Heino, Anni, ed. *Talking to Kinky and Karlheinz: 170 Musicians Get Vocal on* The Music Show. Sydney: ABC Books, 2008.

Hogwood, Christopher. *Music at Court*. London: Folio Society, 1977.

Kidson, Frank. *Traditional Tunes: A Collection of Ballad Airs*. Oxford: Chas. Taphouse & Son, 1891.

Lajosi, Krisztina and Andreas Stynen, eds. *Choral Societies and Nationalism in Europe*. Leiden: Brill, 2015.

Lewisohn, Mark. *Tune In: The Beatles: All These Years, Vol. 1*. London: Little, Brown, 2013.

Low, Tim. *Where Song Began: Australia's Birds and How They Changed the World*. Melbourne: Penguin, 2014.

McCarthy, Kerry. *Byrd*. New York: Oxford University Press, 2020.

McCarthy, Kerry. *Tallis*. New York: Oxford University Press, 2020.

Mackerras, Colin. *The Rise of the Peking Opera, 1770–1870*. Oxford: Clarendon, 1972.

McIlvenna, Una. *Singing the News of Death: Execution Ballads in Europe 1500–1900*. New York: Oxford University Press, 2022.

Maddocks, Fiona. *Hildegard of Bingen: The Woman of Her Age*. London: Faber, 2013.

Marcus, Greil. *Invisible Republic: Bob Dylan's Basement Tapes*. London: Picador, 1997.

Marcus, Greil. *Three Songs, Three Singers, Three Nations*. Cambridge, MA: Harvard University Press, 2015.

Massey, Reginald and Jamila Massey. *The Music of India*. London: Kahn & Averill, 1976.

Mellers, Wilfrid. *Bach and the Dance of God*. London: Faber, 1980.

Mellers, Wilfrid. *Beethoven and the Voice of God*. London: Faber, 1983.

Molleson, Kate. *Sound Within Sound: Opening Our Ears to the Twentieth Century*. London: Faber, 2022.

Moskovitz, Marc D. *Measure: In Pursuit of Musical Time*. Woodbridge: Boydell Press, 2022.

Neal, Mark Anthony. *Black Ephemera: The Crisis and Challenge of the Musical Archive*. New York: New York University Press, 2022.

Neale, Margo and Lynne Kelly, eds. *Songlines: The Power and Promise*. Port Melbourne: Thames & Hudson, 2020.

Oakley, Giles. *The Devil's Music: A History of the Blues*. London: British Broadcasting Corporation, 1976.

Packer, Renée Levine and Mary Jane Leach. *Gay Guerrilla: Julius Eastman and His Music*. Rochester, NY: University of Rochester Press, 2015.

Pinker, Steven. *How the Mind Works*. New York: W.W. Norton & Co, 1997.

Provine, Robert C., Yosihiko Tokumaru and J. Lawrence Witzleben, eds. *The Garland Encyclopedia of World Music, Vol. 7: East Asia: China, Japan, and Korea*. New York: Routledge, 2002.

Reaney, Gilbert. *Machaut*. London: Oxford University Press, 1971.

Ritz, David. *Divided Soul: The Life of Marvin Gaye*. New York: Da Capo, 2010.

Rosen, Charles. *Freedom and the Arts: Essays on Music and Literature*. Cambridge, MA: Harvard University Press, 2012.

Ross, Alex. *The Rest Is Noise: Listening to the Twentieth Century*. New York: Farrar, Straus & Giroux, 2007.

Ross, Alex. *Wagnerism: Art and Politics in the Shadow of Music*. New York: Farrar, Straus & Giroux, 2020.

Schafer, Murray. *British Composers in Interview*. London: Faber, 1963.

Schuller, Gunther. *Musings: The Musical Worlds of Gunther Schuller*. New York: Oxford University Press, 1986.

Skeaping, Lucy. *Broadside Ballads: Songs from the Streets, Taverns, Theatres and Countryside of Seventeenth-Century England*. London: Faber Music, 2005.

Stefaniak, Alexander. *Becoming Clara Schumann: Performance Strategies and Aesthetics in the Culture of the Musical Canon*. Bloomington: Indiana University Press, 2021.

Stone, Ruth M., ed. *The Garland Encyclopedia of World Music, Vol. 1: Africa*. New York: Routledge, 1998.

Strunk, Oliver. *Source Readings in Music History*, revised edition. New York: W.W. Norton & Co., 1998.

Taruskin, Richard. *Stravinsky and the Russian Traditions: A Biography of the Works Through Mavra*. Berkeley: University of California Press, 1996.

Taruskin, Richard. *The Oxford History of Western Music*. New York: Oxford University Press, 2005.

Tenzer, Michael and John Roeder, eds. *Analytical and Cross-Cultural Studies in World Music*. New York: Oxford University Press, 2011.

Tick, Judith. *Ruth Crawford Seeger: A Composer's Search for American Music*. New York: Oxford University Press, 1997.

Tomlinson, Gary. *A Million Years of Music: The Emergence of Human Modernity*. New York: Zone Books, 2018.

Tucker, Mark, ed. *The Duke Ellington Reader*. New York: Oxford University Press, 1993.

Wierzbicki, James. *When Music Mattered: American Music in the Sixties*. New York: Palgrave, 2022.

Wilson, Thomas A., ed. *On Sacred Grounds: Culture, Society, Politics, and the Formation of the Cult of Confucius*. Cambridge, MA: Harvard University Asia Center, 2002.

Wood, James. *Tapping the Source*. London: Vision Edition, 2022.

Acknowledgements

For comments and suggestions, specific and general, critical, sympathetic and encouraging, I thank A.J. America, Philip Bailey, William Barton, Linda Barwick, Ce Benedict, Martin Buzacott, Rachel Campbell, Maureen Cooney, Felix Cross, Robert Davidson, Brett Dean, Jim Denley, Graham Devlin, Helen English, Anna Goldsworthy, Paul Grabowsky, Catherine Ingram, Xing Jin, Ann Jones, Richard Langham Smith, David Larkin, Riley Lee, Lu Liu, Kate Lloyd, Penny Lomax, Kate and Don Munro, Karl Neuenfeldt, Kirsty Newton, Ellie Parnell, Roland Peelman, Gelareh Pour, Tim Pye, Mahesh Radhakrishnan, Brian Ritchie, Josh Robinson, Josh Stenberg, Cathy Strickland, Joseph Tawadros, Judith Tick, Joseph Toltz, Dom Turner, Belinda Webster, Kim Williams, Elizabeth Wood and Kezia Yap.

I am grateful to the Gay'wu Group of Women for permission to quote from their remarkable book, *Songspirals*.

I particularly want to thank Chris Feik of Black Inc. for asking me to write this book – I don't believe I hesitated more than half an hour; Denise O'Dea for her customarily tasteful editing of the manuscript; my colleagues at ABC Radio National for allowing me the time to write it; and my wife and daughter, the book's dedicatees, for putting up with me while I did.

Image Credits

Every effort has been made to contact the copyright holders of material in this book. However, where an omission has occurred, the publisher will gladly include acknowledgement in any future edition.

p. 16: Collection of Museum of Prehistory Blaubeuren. Photograph by Tomatenpflanze. Image via Wikimedia Commons.

p. 17: Photograph by Gary Todd. Image via Wikimedia Commons.

p. 19: Charles K. Wilkinson, *Female Musicians*, facsimile 1921–1922; original c. 1400–1390 BCE. Held in The Met Museum, Rogers Fund, 1930. Image via The Met.

p. 20: Justin Kerr via Mayavase Database.

p. 22: Hiroyuki Ito / Hulton Archive / Getty Images.

p. 25: Photographer unknown. Image via Chewtoy / Last.fm.

p. 26: Photographer unknown, 1900s. Held in the Jill Rosemary Dias Collection. Image via Wikimedia Commons.

p. 50: Lebrecht Music & Arts / Alamy Stock Photo

p. 52: © Bodleian Libraries, University of Oxford.

p. 53: Photograph by the European Shakuhachi Society. Image via Wikimedia Commons.

p. 54: Collection of Ghent University Library. Image via Wikimedia Commons.

p. 60: Illustration by Aira Pimping.

p. 66: Johann Sebastian Bach, 'Ricercar a 6' BWV 1079, 1747. Held in the Berlin State Library, Germany.

p. 71: Lorenzo Costa, *The Concert*, c. 1488–90, oil on wood, 95.3 × 75.6 cm. Held in the collection of the National Gallery, UK, Salting Bequest, 1910. Photograph by Sailko. Image via Wikimedia Commons.

p. 73: Image via Dreweatts Online / Auctionet.com.

p. 76: *Black Angels* by George Crumb © 1971 C.F. Peters Corporation, New York. Reproduced by permission of Faber Music Ltd. All Rights Reserved.

p. 84: The cover of Scott Joplin, *Maple Leaf Rag*, first edition, 1899. Image via Library of Congress / Wikimedia Commons.

p. 90: Photographer unknown. Held in John Edwards Memorial Foundation Records (PF-20001), Southern Folklife Collection, Wilson Library. Image via Wikimedia Commons.

p. 93: Photograph by Engineer J.A.L. Horn, 1935. Image via National Museum of Denmark / Flickr.

p. 99: Photograph by Péter Szvitek. Image via Wikimedia Commons / Indafotó. Alteration made: black and white.

p. 103: Unknown photographer, 1904. Image via https://theoryofmusic.wordpress.com/

p. 115: Creator unknown, 1924–39. Image via Samuel Coleridge-Taylor Foundation.

p. 120: PALM/RSCH / Redferns / Getty Images.

p. 138: *4'33"* by John Cage © 1960 Henmar Press, Inc., New York. Reproduced by permission of Faber Music Ltd. All Rights Reserved

p. 143: Illustration held in the collection of the Library of Congress. Courtesy Judith Tick.

p. 144: Photograph by Josef Albert, 1865. Image via Wikimedia Commons.

p. 145: Photographer unknown, 1913. Image via Wikimedia Commons.

p. 168: Photographer unknown. Image courtesy of Hogan Jazz Archive.

p. 185: Reproduced by permission of Annea Lockwood. Photograph by Geoff Adams.

p. 188: NYPL / Science Source / Science Photo Library.

p. 195: Photograph by Harris & Ewing, 9 February 1916. Held in the collection of Library of Congress. Image via Wikimedia Commons.

p. 197: Photographer unknown. Smithsonian Center for Folklife and Cultural Heritage, Smithsonian Institution.

p. 203: © Yves Arman / Fondation A.R.M.A.N. Reproduced with permission.

Index

42nd Street (film) 129

aak (Korean court music) 23, 41, 164
Adventures of Robin Hood, The (film) 128
Aelred of Riveaux 147
  Speculum caritatis 147
akonting 26, 27
al-Shushtari, Abu al-Hasan 138
Albigensian Crusade 94, 178
'All the Things You Are', 174
Allen, Fulton (see Fuller, Blind Boy)
Altenberg, Peter 158
American Musician and Arts Journal 84
Andrews, Julie 52
Animal Farm (film) 181
Animals, the 196
archaeology, musical finds in 8–9, 10, 11, 15–20
Arlen, Harold 181
Armstrong, Louis 65, 139, 169, 170, 171, 174
  Hot Sevens 65, 170
  plays cornet for Bessie Smith on 'Saint Louis Blues', 194
  Potato Head Blues', 65, 199, 200
arhoolies 40–1
Aristotle 11, 12, 15
  Politics 15
Artusi, Giovanni Maria 150
  On the Imperfections of Modern Music 150
Ashbery, John 10
Atherton, Michael 81
Auden, Wystan Hugh 48, 174
  'The Age of Anxiety', 174
Austen, Jane 106
Axton, Mae Boren 134
Ayler, Albert 173
Aztec music 20
Bach, Johann Sebastian 2, 3, 64, 66–7, 69, 72, 83, 86, 102, 124, 126, 127, 140, 146, 159, 176
  Art of Fugue, The 164
  Brandenburg Concertos 69
  chorales 3, 4
  keyboard music 65, 121
  Musical Offering, The 66–7, 86
  Saint Matthew Passion 78
  Well-tempered Clavier, The 64
Bacharach, Burt 111
Bailey, Philip 82–3
Ballets Russes 156
banjo 26–8, 40
Barbieri, Gato 200
Barnum, Phineas Taylor 118
Bartók, Béla 3, 83, 104, 139, 142, 165–66, 193
  Allegro barbaro 166
  String Quartet No 3, 76
Barton, William 1, 4, 209–10
  'Kalkadunga Yurdu', 209–10
  Kalkadungu (with Matthew Hindson) 209
  Square Circles Beneath Red Desert Sand 209
Basement Jaxx 209
Basie, Count 140, 164
Bayreuth Festival 74,118
BBC Symphony Orchestra 126
Beach Boys, the 200
  Pet Sounds 200
Beatles, the 85, 130, 191, 198, 200
  'Love Me Do', 86
  perform 'Freight Train', 198
  Please Please Me 200
  Revolver 200
  Sgt Pepper's Lonely Hearts Club Band 200, 202
bebop (see under Jazz)
Beecham, Thomas 113

Beethoven, Ludwig van 2, 67, 72–3, 78, 102, 107–08, 123, 124–25, 126, 127, 140, 146, 159, 160, 169, 179
metronome, adoption of 72–3
Grosse Fuge Op. 133, 145, 170
piano music 70, 85, 121
Piano Sonata in C sharp minor Op. 27, no 2 (*Moonlight*) 76, 86
Piano Sonata in F minor Op. 57 (*Appassionata*) 125, 179
Piano Sonata in B flat Op. 106 (*Hammerklavier*) 108
Piano Sonata in C minor, Op. 111, 145
string quartets 107, 164
symphonies 67, 73, 107, 169, 190
Symphony No 3 in E flat Op. 55 (*Eroica*) 107
Symphony No 5 in C minor Op. 67, 124, 166–67, 190
Symphony No 9 in D minor Op. 125, 125, 179
Violin Concerto in D Op. 61, 119–20
Bellini, Vincenzo 118, 121, 153
Il Pirata 121
Beowulf 33
Berg, Alban 142, 143, 158, 160
Five Orchestral Songs after Postcards by Peter Altenberg 158–59
Lyric Suite 142–43
Berio, Luciano 149
Berlin, Irving 181
Berlin Philharmonic 127, 188, 209
Berlin State Opera 127
Berlioz, Hector 2, 104, 124, 140, 167
operas 67
Berry, Chuck 134
Bhosle, Asha 129–30
bianzhong bells 17–18
Black Dyke (Mills) Band 82
Blake, Blind (Arthur) 90
Blake, William 33–4
Songs of Innocence and of Experience 34
Bley, Carla 91, 200
Escalator Over the Hill 200
'Blue Suede Shoes',
bluegrass 28
blues 44, 89–91, 133–34, 191, 193–98
Chicago blues 195
Delta blues 193
origins and development of 193–98
Piedmont blues 89, 90
Bob and Marcia 176
Bolden, Charles 'Buddy', 168–69
Bollywood (see Hindi cinema)
Bote & Bock 106
Boulanger, Lili 110–11
D'un soir triste 111
Boulanger, Nadia 110, 111
Boulez, Pierre 74, 139, 158, 159, 164, 173, 183
conducts *Parsifal* 74
Le Marteau sans maître 144
Piano Sonata No 2, 170
Structures 1a 183
Bowlly, Al 85
Brahms, Johannes 2, 3, 73, 102, 103, 121, 124, 125, 127, 140, 142, 159
Symphony No 1 in C minor Op. 68, 125
brass bands 82–3
Brendel, Franz 122
Bride of Frankenstein 128
Brief Encounter (film) 130
Brighouse and Rastrick Band 82
British Broadcasting Corporation (BBC) 187
Brodsky Quartet 209
Broonzy, Big Bill 192
Brontë sisters 106
Bruce, Jack 200
Bruckner, Anton 103
symphonies 67
Buddhist chant 38
Bull City Red 91
Burkholder, J. Peter 123
Burns, Robert 34
Burrundi, Royal Drummers of 31–2
Byrd, William 80
Byron, Lord 57
Don Juan 57
Byzantine chant 50

C-Pop 135
Caccini, Francesca 109, 112
Caccini, Giulio 109
cadence calls 40–1
Cage, John 137–38, 139, 183, 205
4'33", 137–38, 145–46, 183–84
definition of music 205

Cairo Symphony Orchestra 78
calypso 29, 40–1, 95,
Captains Courageous (film) 128
Carlisle, Elsie 85
Carlos, Wendy 127
  Switched on Bach 127
Carnegie Hall (New York) 165, 209
Carter, Betty 131
Carter, Elliott 111, 165, 181
  Holiday Overture 165
  promoted by the CIA 181
  String Quartet No 1, 181
Carthy, Martin 44
Casablanca (film) 128
Cerdan, Marcel 132
Chaminade, Cécile 110
  Flute Concertino in D Op. 107, 110
Cherry, Don 200
Chicago Symphony Orchestra 110
China Musical Instrument Association 79
Chinese opera (see xiqu)
Chishti order 37
Chopin, Frédéric 2, 45, 103, 146
  Piano Sonata No 2 in B flat minor 45
choral societies 81–3
Christian Ludwig, Margrave of Brandenburg 69
Chronicles, Second Book of 96
Chrysander, Friedrich 124
CIA (Central Intelligence Agency) as patron of the arts 181
Clement, Franz 120
Cobham, Billy 201
Coleman, Emil 85
Coleman, Ornette 170, 173–74
  The Shape of Jazz to Come 174
Coleridge-Taylor, Samuel 114–16
  Hiawatha's Wedding Feast 114, 115, 116
  The Song of Hiawatha 114, 116
Coltrane, John 86, 173
  A Love Supreme 86
Concert de la Loge Olympique, Le 100–01
Concert Spirituel 117
Confucius 21
  Analects 21
Copland, Aaron 111
Corea, Chick 201
Costa, Lorenzo 71, 72
Costello, Elvis 183
Cotten, Elizabeth 196–98, 209–10
  Folksongs and Instrumentals with Guitar 198
  'Freight Train', 197, 198, 209–10
country music (American) 7
Couperin, François 124
Covent Garden, Royal Opera House (London) 112, 113
Crawford Seeger, Ruth 142–44, 197
  String Quartet 67, 142–44
'Crazy Blues', 194
Cream 200
Croce, Benedetto 4
Crosby, Bing 130
Crumb, George 75
  Black Angels 76, 177
Cultural Revolution (China) 78–9, 179
cumbia 28
Curtis Institute of Music (Philadelphia) 176
Czerny, Carl 108

Đại Việt court 1–2, 23–4
  Cham singers at 1, 24
David, King of Israel 5, 96–7
Davis, Reverend Gary 90
Davis, Miles 174–75, 183, 201–02
  'Birth of the Cool' sessions 183
  Bitches Brew 201
  In a Silent Way 201
  Kind of Blue 183, 201
Davies, Iva 209
Davies, Peter Maxwell 172
  Eight Songs for a Mad King 172–73
'Death Letter', 196
Debussy, Claude 3, 77, 78, 79, 84, 103, 140, 159, 163, 164, 199
  Prélude à l'après-midi d'un faune 159
DeJohnette, Jack 201
Delius, Frederick 199
Densmore, Frances 193, 195, 208
Deutsche Grammophon 188
Diaghilev, Sergei 156
didgeridoo 1, 42–3
  Aboriginal names for 1
d'Indy, Vincent 124
Disney, Walt 129
Dodds, Johnny 65, 170
Dodds, Warren 'Baby' 170

đông sơn drums 17
DownBeat (magazine) 199
Donizetti, Gaetano 118, 153
'Dublin Bay', 192
Duel in the Sun 128
Dutilleux, Henri 111
Durden, Tommy 134
Dvořák, Antonin 2, 102, 116, 127–28
  Symphony No 9 in E (*From the New World*) 128

Eastman, Julius 171–73
  Crazy Nigger 172
  Evil Nigger 172
  Gay Guerilla 172
  Nigger Faggot 172
Eberle, Ray 127
Egypt (ancient) music in 18–19, 39, 71
Eibingen, Abbey of 2
Einstein, Albert 161
El-Dabh, Halim 202, 210
  Ta'abir al-Zār 202
Elgar, Edward 2, 103, 114, 140
  Cello Concerto in E minor, Op. 85, 187
  The Dream of Gerontius 114
electric guitar, invention of,, 189
electronic dance music (EDM) 135, 169
Eliot, George (Mary Ann Evans) 106
  Middlemarch 106
Eliot, Thomas Stearns 139, 210
  Four Quartets 210
Elizabeth I, Queen of England 56, 79–80
Ellington, Duke 139, 140, 164, 198–200
  Black, Brown and Beige 199
  'Reminiscing in Tempo', 198–99
  Sacred Concerts 199
Eminem 34
Esterháza 2, 99, 100, 101
Esterházy, Anton 101, 102
Esterházy, Nikolaus I 99–101
Esterházy, Nikolaus II 102
E.T. The Extra-Terrestrial 129
'Etenraku', 22–3
Evans, Bill 182
Exodus, Book of 14

Fantasia (film) 129
Farid, Ibn al-, 38–9
Farrenc, Louise 109
Ferneyhough, Brian 75
field hollers 40–1
film music 112, 128–30, 153, 164
Firnas, Abbas ibn 72
Florentine Camerata 150
folk songs (Western) 41–2, 43–4
Foster, Stephen C., 83–4
  'Beautiful Dreamer', 83
  'Camptown Races, The', 83
  'Hard Times Come again No More', 83
  'Jeannie with the Light Brown Hair', 83
  'Oh! Susanna', 83
Franklin, Aretha 177
Frederick the Great, King of Prussia 67, 86
'Frère Jacques', 66
Fuller, Blind Boy 89–91, 92, 134
  'Step It up and Go', 90, 91
Furtwängler, Wilhelm 127

gagaku (Japanese court music) 21–3, 41, 68, 166
Galás, Diamanda 169
Galileo Galilei 72
gamelan 64–5
Gaskell, Elizabeth 106
Gaye, Marvin 174–75, 177
  What's Going On 177
Gay'wu Group of Women 12–13, 32, 45–6
George, Stefan 160
George V, King of England 116
Géricault, Théodore 171
Gershwin, George 128, 181
  Piano Concerto in F 128
Gewandhaus (Leipzig) 117, 118, 119
Giddens, Rhiannon 27
Gillespie, Dizzy 139, 164, 174
Glass, Philip 111, 139, 172
Glenn Miller Orchestra 127
Gone with the Wind (film) 128
Gonzaga, Vincenzo, Duke of Mantua 151
Goodman, Benny 164, 181
Gorky, Maxim 125
Gould, Glenn 188–89
Goya, Francisco 182
goze 92
Grainger, Percy 8, 192, 193
Greek (ancient) chant 50
griots 95–6, 97, 166
Guevara, Che 171

Guido of Arezzo 51, 54, 78, 87
  Guidonian Hand 51–2, 53

Hafez (Khwāje Shams-od-Dīn Moḥammad Ḥāfeẓ-e) 33
Hammerstein, Oscar (II) 51
Hammond, John 199
Hammonds Saltaire Band 82
Hancock, Herbie 201, 209
Handel, George Frideric 2, 3, 102, 117–18, 124
  Messiah 81, 114
  operas 117–18
Handy, W.C., 194
  'Saint Louis Blues', 194
Hanover Square Rooms 117, 119
Hardin, Lil 170
harps 18
Harrach family 102
Harrison, Beatrice 187
Harry James Orchestra 127
Hathor (Egyptian goddess) 18
Haydn, Joseph 2, 98–102, 107, 123, 140, 146, 160, 164, 166
  baryton trios 99
  Masses 102
  operas 99
  piano sonatas 100
  piano trios 100
  string quartets 81, 100, 107, 166
  symphonies 100–01, 107, 117, 166
  Symphony No 82 in C (*The Bear*) 166
  Symphony No 85 in B flat (*La Reine*) 101
He Luting 79
'Heartbreak Hotel', 133, 134, 188
Hebrew chant 35–6
Heine, Heinrich 121
Hendrix, Jimi 144, 177
  plays 'The Star Spangled Banner' at Woodstock 177
Hensel, Fanny (see Mendelssohn Hensel, Fanny)
Hensel, Wilhelm 105
Henselt, Adolf von 121
Henze, Hans Werner 171
  The Raft of the Medusa 171
Hepburn, Audrey 129
'Here Comes the Bride', 44
Hess, Myra 126
Hildegard of Bingen 2, 56, 146–48, 150, 164, 210
  O ecclesia occuli tui 146
  Ordo Virtutum 150
Hindson, Matthew 209
  Kalkadungu (with William Barton) 209
Hindi cinema 129–30
Hindu chant 35–6, 38, 50–1
Hindustani classical music 7, 139–40
Hines, Earl 170
hip hop 7, 28, 34–5, 135
Hitler, Adolf 179, 180
Ho Chi Minh 171
Hoffman, Al 85
Holiday, Billie 174, 175, 176
Holland, dave 201
Holmès, Augusta 109
Holst, Gustav 129
Homer 33
House, Son 196
  'Death Letter', 196
Howard, Thomas, Duke of Norfolk 56
Howard, Trevor 130
Howlin' Wolf 196
Huddersfield Choral Society 82
Hughes, Robert 139
Huizong of Song, Chinese Emperor 23
Hurrian Hymns 49
'Hymn to Nikkal', 49–50

Icehouse 209
India, Symphony Orchestra of 78
Industrial Revolution 81
Islamic attitudes to music 36–8
Italian Gramophone Company (HMV) 131
It's a Wonderful Life 128
Ives, Charles 68, 163
  Symphony No 4, 68

J-Pop 135
Jacquet de La Guerre, Elisabeth 109
Jara, Victor 178
Jaws 129
jazz 131, 164–65, 167–69, 191, 193
  bebop 139, 140, 164, 165, 183
  big band swing 140, 162–63, 164
  cool jazz 183

free jazz 173–74, 183
Nazi restrictions on 182
jazz (*cont.*)
origins and development of 2, 167–69, 193–94
recording 131, 168–69, 194, 198–201
Jefferson, Blind Lemon 90, 194
'Long Lonesome Blues', 194
Johnson, Blind Willie 90
Johnson, Celia 130
Johnson, Robert 120
Jones, Paul 200
Jones, Quincy 111
Jones, Rickie Lee 183
jongo 28
Joplin, Scott 84–5
'Maple Leaf Rag', 84
Treemonisha 84
Jordan, Sheila 200
Joyce, Eileen 130
Joyce, James 139
Judith, Book of 56

K-Pop 135
kaiso 29
Kampala Symphony Orchestra 78
Kandinsky, Wassily 139
Karajan, Herbert von 178, 188
Keita, Salif 96, 191
Kern, Jerome 174
Kerr, Deborah 129
Khan, Nusrat Fateh Ali 37
Khusrau, Amīr 2, 37
Kimbanguist Symphony Orchestra 78
Kidson, Frank 45
King, Martin Luther (Jr) *167*
King and I, The (film) 129
King Kong (film) 128
King's Row (film) 128
Knappertsbusch, Hans 74
kobzari 92
Koller, Maria 102
komusō 93–4
kora 26, 33
Korea, State Symphony Orchestra of the Democratic People's Republic of 78
Korngold, Erich Wolfgang 128, 129
koto 24
Kulthum, Umm 131, 132

Lean, David 130
Lenin, Vladimir Ilych 125, 179
Lennon, John 198
Léonin 145, 147, 148–49, 170
Viderunt omnes 145
Levi, Hermann 74
Lind, Jenny 118
Liszt, Franz 2, 102, 108, 120–21, 122, 128, 142
piano music 67
'Little Man You've Had a Busy Day', 85
Little Richard 134
Little Walter 196
Little Women (film) 128
Lockwood, Annea 184–85
'piano burning', 184–85
Piano Transplants 184
Lomax, Alan 193
Lone Ranger, The (TV) 130
Longfellow, Henry Wadsworth 114
Lost Horizon (film) 128
Louis XIV, King of France 97
Lourié, Arthur 180
'Love Me Do', 86
Lozi drumming 32
Lu Hongen 79
Luca della Robbia 71–2
lullabies 5, 38–41, 208
Lully, Jean-Baptiste 97–8
lutes 25–6
lyres 18
Lutyens, Elisabeth 111–12, 113, 164
film scores 112, 164
Lý Thái Tông 1–2, 24

Ma, Yo-Yo 209
Maal, Baaba 96
Macero, Teo 201–02
Machaut, Guillaume de 55
Ma fin est mon commencement 55–6
Maelzel, Johann Nepomuk 72, 73
Mahābhārata 33
Mahler, Alma 160
Mahler, Gustav 74–5, 103, 128
symphonies 67, 75
Symphony No 8 in E flat 76
Symphony No 10 in F sharp 144

mambo 28
Mao Zedong 78, 79
Marcus, Greil 193
mariachi 94–5
Marie Antoinette 101
Mariinsky Theatre (St Petersburg) 209
Marsalis, Wynton 4
Martin, Tony 127
Marx, A.B., 14
Matisse, Henri 139
Matoub, Lounès 178
Mayan music 19–20
McDevitt, Chas 198
McLaughlin, John 201
McTell, Blind Willie 90
Mendelssohn, Abraham 104
Mendelssohn, Felix 2, 45, 104–06, 118, 140
 concertos 105
 Midsummer Night's Dream (Wedding March) 45
 piano music 105
 songs 105
 symphonies 105
 St Paul 81
Mendelssohn, Moses 104
Mendelssohn Hensel, Fanny 104–06, 108
 identity uncovered by Queen Victoria 105
 'Italien', 105
 6 Lieder, op. 1, 106
 piano music 105
 songs 105
Menuhin, Yehudi 82–3, 139
Merman, Ethel 190
Merzbow (Masami Akita) 170
Mesopotamia, music in 39, 41
metronome 72–3
Metropolitan Opera, New York 113, 128
Mevlevi order (whirling dervishes) 36–7
Mexican Revolution 95
milkarri 13, 46
minnesingers 94
minstrel shows 27, 83
Mitropoulos, Dimitri 1165
Molière (Jean-Baptiste Poquelin) 97
Mondrian, Piet 139
Monteverdi, Claudio 140, 150–52, 153, 156, 171
 madrigals 145, 151
 L'incoronazione di Poppea 151–52
 L'Orfeo 68–9, 150–51, 185
'Moon Love', 127
Moore, Thomas 34
Morning Chronicle, the 101
Morrison, Toni 175–76
Mosolov, Alexander 180
 The Iron Foundry 180
Motown Records 177
Mozart, Wolfgang Amadeus 2, 68, 102, 118, 123, 127, 140, 160
 operas 118, 153
 string quartets 81
 Symphony No 40 in G minor K. 550, 155
 Symphony No 41 in C K. 551 (*Jupiter*) 68
Mountain Chief (Blackfoot/South Piegan) 195
Muddy Waters 196
Mulligan, Gerry 183
Musgrave, Thea 111
music notation 18–19, 22, 41, 47–87 (passim)
musicology 124
musique concrète 202–03
Musikverein (Vienna) 158–59
'My Black Mama', 196
My Fair Lady (film) 129

Nancarrow, Conlon 67
NBC Symphony Orchestra 126
N'Dour, Youssou 96, 191
Nero, Emperor of Rome 152
New York Philharmonic Orchestra 128, 173
Newton, Isaac 161
nhã nhạc (Vietnamese court music) 23–4
Nixon, Marni 129
noise art 169–70
Nono, Luigi 164, 170–71
 Il canto sospeso 164
notation (see music notation)
Notre-Dame, School of 97, 145, 148–49

O'Carolan, Turlough 92
Odyssey (Homer) 33
Ogny, Comte d', 100–01
Oliveros, Pauline 75
Orff, Carl 180
 attempts to interest Third Reich in *Schulwerk* 180

Carmina Burana 180
Original Dixieland Jass Band 168–69, 194
'Livery Stable Blues', 168, 169
Orwell, George 181
Ory, Kid 170

Paganini, Niccolò 120, 121
Palestrina, Giovanni Pierluigi da 65
Park Chung Hee 178
Parker, Charlie 131, 139, 144, 164, 170, 174
'Bird of Paradise', 174
'Hothouse', 174
'Ornithology', 131
Parker, 'Colonel' Tom 133, 134
Performing Right Society (UK) 116
Perkins, Carl 134
'Blue Suede Shoes', 133, 134
Perlman, Itzhak 117
Pérotin 148–49
Peru, National Symphony Orchestra of 78
Peters, Edition (music publisher) 138, 145–46
Peyton Place (TV) 130
Phillips, Tom 75
Piaf, Edith 131–32
'Non, je ne regrette rien', 132
piano 79, 81
as recital instrument 2, 70–1,
as singalong instrument 83, 85
destroyed in the Cultural Revolution 79
in extremis (set on fire/pushed through walls) 184–85
ubiquity of 81
virtuoso repertoire for 108, 120–22
Picasso, Pablo 139, 170
Pinker, Steven 10–11, 12, 13, 36, 206
Pinochet, Augusto 178
plainsong (plainchant) 35, 51, 54
Plato 11, 12
Laws 12
The Republic 12
Poppaea Sabina, Empress of Rome 152
Porter, Cole 174
'Potato Head Blues', 65, 199, 200
Powell, Bud 139
Pound, Ezra 138
Presley, Elvis 130, 133–34, 188
Price, Florence 110
Symphony No 1 in E minor 110
Prokofiev, Sergei 129, 180–81
On Guard for Peace 180–81
Promenade Concerts (London) 113
Psalms, Book of 138
punk rock 140, 170, 183
Pythagoras 11-12

qawwali 2, 37–8
Qur'ān 36
recitation of 35–6

Rachmaninoff, Sergei 128, 162
Piano Concerto No 2 in C minor 130
contemporary popularity of 162
Radigue, Eliane 202–03, 204
Trilogie de la mort 203
Rainey, Gertrude 'Ma', 194
Ramayana 33
Rameau, Jean-Philippe 124
Randafison, Sylvestre 25
rap 34–5
'Rapper's Delight', 34, 210
Ravel, Maurice 3, 104, 157
Rawhide (TV program) 130
Ray Noble Orchestra 85
RCA Victor 133, 134, 188
Rebecca (film) 128
recorded music 130–35, 168–69, 187–204
Reich, Steve 172
Rig Veda 50–1
Riley, Terry 172
In C 172
Rimsky-Kosakov, Nicolai 156
Rios, Walter de los 127
Sinfonias 127
ritual, music in 31–3
rock and roll 139, 189
Rodgers, Richard 51
Rolling Stones, the 196
Ronstadt, Linda 200
Roosevelt, Theodore 115
Roslavets, Nikolai 180
Rossini, Gioachino 130
Overture to *William Tell* 130
'Row, Row, Row your Boat', 66
Rubens, Peter Paul 151

rumba (Congolese) 29
rumba (Cuban) 28, 29
Rumi, Jalāl ad-Dīn Muḥammad 33, 36, 37
Ruskin, John 167

Saint-Georges, Joseph Bologne, Chevalier de 100–01
'Saint Louis Blues', 194
Saint Mark's Basilica (Venice) 151
Saint-Saëns, Camille 124
Salomon, Johann Peter 101, 117
samba 28
Samuel, Book of 97
sargam 52
Sassoon, Siegfried 206, 207
 'Everyone Sang', 206, 207
Satie, Erik 84–5
Saul, King of Israel 97
Sax, Adolph 189
Schaeffer, Pierre 202
Schafer, R. Murray 111
Schnabel, Artur 70, 71, 76–7, 85
Schoenberg, Arnold 3, 103, 112, 139, 140, 142, 158, 159–62, 163, 183
 String Quartet No 2, 160
 Variations for Orchestra Op. 31, 188
Schubert, Franz 2, 102, 127, 159
Schumann, Clara 2, 109, 120, 121–22
 Variations de concert sur la cavatine du Pirate de Bellini 121
Schumann, Robert 2, 67, 103, 122
 piano music 67
Sea Wolf, The 128
Second Viennese school 160–61
Seeger, Charles 197
Seeger, Mike 198
Seeger, Peggy 197–98
Seeger, Pete 197
Seeger, Ruth Crawford (see Crawford Seeger, Ruth)
Seneca 152
Shakespeare, William 44, 101
shakuhachi 24,
 played by komuso,
 notation 53, 68
Shakur, Tupac 34
Shanghai Conservatory of Music 79
Shanghai Symphony Orchestra 79
Shankar, Ravi 139–40
shanties 40–1
Shaw, Artie 164, 181
Shelley, Percy Bysshe 4
Shields, Larry 169
Shijing 33
shofar 14
Shorter, Wayne 201
Shostakovich, Dimitri 180–81
 The Sun Shines Over the Motherland 181
Sibelius, Jean 2, 104, 162
 contemporary popularity of 162
 piano music 188
Sigler, Maurice 85
Simón Bolivar Symphony Orchestra 78
Simone, Nina 176
 'Mississippi Goddam', 176
 'To Be Young, Gifted and Black', 176
Sinatra, Frank 127, 174, 190
slave trade (Atlantic) 27–9
Smetana, Bedřich 102, 116
Smith, Bessie 194
 'Saint Louis Blues', 194
Smith, Mamie 194
 'Crazy Blues', 194
Smyth, Ethel 112–13, 114, 116
 Der Wald 113
 The Wreckers 112–13
Snoop Dogg 34
Socrates 11, 12
solfège 51–2, 54
solmisation 51–3
son Cubano 28, 29
songlines 13
songspirals (Yolŋu) 12, 12, 32, 46
'Star-Spangled Banner, The', 177
Star Wars 129, 153
Stein, Gertrude 139
Steiner, Max 128, 129
Stockhausen, Karlheinz 75, 139, 164, 178
 Kreuzspiel 164
Stokowski, Leopold 22
'Story of a Starry Night, The', 127
'Strange Fruit', 174, 175
Straus, Oscar 158
 The Chocolate Soldier 158
Strauss, Richard 102, 113, 128
Stravinsky, Igor 3, 67, 85, 102, 129, 139, 140, 145, 156–58, 163, 171, 178, 182
 Firebird, The 156

Petrushka 156
Stravinsky, Igor (*cont.*)
Rite of Spring, The 129, 145, 146, 156–58, 159, 165, 166, 169, 170
Striggio, Alessandro 56
Strozzi, Barbara 109, 112
Strozzi, Giulio 109
Sufism 36–8
Sugarhill Gang, the 34, 210
'Rapper's Delight', 34, 210
Sun Studio (Memphis) 133
Swingle Singers, the 127
Jazz Sébastian Bach 127
Sydney Opera House 146
symphony orchestra, constitution of 29–31, 68
Syrian National Symphony Orchestra 78

tablature 53–4
Takemitsu, Tōru 77–8, 205, 206
November Steps 77
Tallis, Thomas 2, 48, 56, 63, 80
Spem in alium 2, 47–8, 56–7, 63, 65
taonga pūoro 42
Taruskin, Richard 152
Tchaikovsky, Pyotr Ilych 2, 104, 127, 128, 142
Piano Concerto No 1 in B flat minor Op. 23, 127, 141–42
Sleeping Beauty, The 156
Swan Lake 156
Symphony No 5 in E minor, Op. 64, 127
Symphony No 6 in B minor, Op. 74, 127
Teatro San Cassiano (Venice) 151
Terry, Sonny 90–1
Thalberg, Sigismond 121
Tharpe, Sister Rosetta 189
'This Little Light of Mine', 91
Thomas, L.V. (Elvie) 193
Three Tenors, the 118
Tibetan Book of the Dead, The 203
Tiomkin, Dimitri 128, 130
'Tonight We Love', 127
Toscanini, Arturo 126
trobairitz 94
troubadours 94, 95, 178
trouvères 94
Turgenev, Ivan 110
Tutankhamun, Pharaoh of Egypt 18
'Two Sisters, The' (ballad) 93
Ustvolskaya, Galina 181

Vai, Steve 86–7
valiha 24–5
Verdi, Giuseppe 2, 103, 118, 119
Aida 119
Ernani 131
Il trovatore 119
Macbeth 119
Nabucco 119
operas 67, 118
Viardot, Pauline 109
operas 110
Victor Emanuel II, King of Italy 119
Victoria, Queen of England 105
Vietnam Symphony Orchestra 78
Vivaldi, Antonio 69
Four Seasons 69–70

Wagner, Richard 2, 74, 100, 103, 113, 118, 119, 124–25, 128, 129, 140, 153–56, 171, 179–80
Lohengrin 44
operas 67, 118, 153
Parsifal 74
Ring des Nibelungen, Der 119, 153–54
Tristan und Isolde 144, 145, 154–56, 159–60
Wainwright, Harriet 109
Walton, William 129
Waxman, Franz 128, 130
'Way You Look Tonight, The', 131
Wayne, Mabel 85
'Little Man You've Had a Busy Day', 85
Webern, Anton 139, 160, 161, 162, 163, 164
Six Bagatelles Op. 9, 144, 161, 162
Six Pieces for Orchestra Op. 6, 159
Webster, Ben 174
Weill, Kurt 200
Wen of Sui, Chinese Emperor 23
West Side Story (film) 129
'What Is This Thing Called Love?', 174
whirling dervishes (see Mevlevi order)
Whiskey, Nancy 198
Wiley, Geeshie 193
Wilkinson, Thomas 207
Williams, John 129, 153

Williams, Mary Lou 139
Williams, Tony 201
Wolf, Hugo 164
women composers in Western art music 3, 104–13
work songs 38–41
Wood, Natalie 129
Woodstock Festival 177
Woolf, Virginia 41, 139
  A Room of One's Own 41
Wordsworth, William 206, 207
  'The Solitary Reaper', 206, 207

Xenakis, Iannis 68
xiao 24
xiqu 149–50

yǎyue (Chinese court music) 20–1, 23, 41, 97, 164
Yi of Zeng, Marquis 17, 18
Young, La Monte 75
  Piano Piece #1 for Terry Riley 184
Yun, Isang 77, 177–78
  Réak 77, 177

Zappa, Frank 86–7
  The Frank Zappa Guitar Book 86–7
  Hot Rats 86
  'While you Were Out', 86–7
Zawinul, Joe 201
zheng,24
zithers 18, 24, 25

READ IN A DAY.
REMEMBER FOR A LIFETIME.

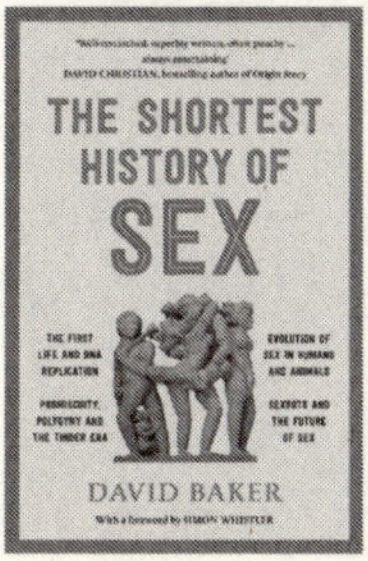